What Dolls Wore Before

Doll Costumes and Accessories, 1850 - 1925

Florence Theriault

Gold Horse Publishing

© Copyright 1997 Theriault's Gold Horse Publishing.
All rights reserved. No part of this book may be reproduced in any form or by any means, electronic or mechanical, including photocopying, recording or by an informationretreival system without permission from the Publisher.

To order additional copies:
Dollmasters, PO Box 2319, Annapolis, Maryland 21404
Tel. 410-224-4386 Fax 410-224-2515

Special thank you to Natalie Stewart

Art Direction and Design: David W. Hirner
Photography: Gwin Hunt

$39
ISBN: 0-912823-70-4
Printed in Hong Kong

Contents

Introduction
4

Chapter I
Early Fashion Costumes, 1830 - 1855
7

Chapter II
Early Child Doll Dresses, 1860 - 1875
17

Chapter III
The Classic Fashion Doll, 1855-1875
29

Chapter IV
Child or Bebe Doll Dresses, 1875 - 1895
65

Chapter V
Best Dresses, 1880 - 1895
85

Chapter VI
Pinafores and Aprons, 1865 - 1910
107

Chapter VII
Dresses and Playsets, 1890 - 1925
115

Chapter VIII
Chemises and Undergarments, 1870 - 1915
131

Chapter IX
Mariner Costumes, 1880 - 1915
139

Chapter X
Miscellaneous Costumes Including Gentlemens, Occupational and Folklore, 1875 - 1925
148

Introduction

In a survey in the United States in 1911 young girls were asked about their relationships with their dolls. The results were surprising. While 82 girls thought of their dolls chiefly as friends, the largest number of girls, 266, thought first of doll clothing and dressing and undressing their dolls.

The daughters and granddaughters of these 1911 young girls are today's doll collectors, and if you were to ask them what first brought them to doll collecting the answer would likely be as one collector said "I liked to dress dolls."

Nothing really ever changes.

In fact, the history of dolls is inextricably interwoven with the study of costume. The use of the doll as fashion mannequin is well documented in 17th and 18th-century papers. The doll served as model not only for the latest in haute couture, but also as a dimensional form for correct posture, pose and costume draping. Although these traveling mannequins did not actually begin their "life" as play dolls, it is certain that they became so in time.

Until about 1844, however, costumes of commercially-made play dolls were largely for show. Cut from small pieces of fabric for economy purposes, they were tacked directly onto the doll bodies; it is astonishing how, once removed, these gorgeous costumes became simply a mish-mash of puzzle fragments.

In 1844 Simon-Auguste Brouillet introduced a new idea at the Paris Exhibition. He exhibited dolls that could be dressed and undressed. It was an idea that quickly caught on. After all, here was an opportunity for doll firms to expand their existing business. One could not only sell a doll, but one could continue to sell dresses, hats, bonnets, shoes and multitudes of other fineries for that doll.

An entire industry arose, all concerned with dressing the doll. In Paris, London, and later New York and other major cities in the prosperous New World (i.e. new market) of America, the commercial production and sale of doll clothing and accessories was a thriving business from after 1860.

Side-by-side with the development of the commercial doll costume industry, was the continuing use of the doll as model for home sewers. Dressing dolls in clothes wrought by hand was not only an inspirational way to teach one's young daughter to sew, but the doll industry quickly perceived that even this "competition" to their ready-made doll costumes could become profitable. Thus arose throughout the 2nd half of the 19th century a corollary industry related to home-sewing of doll costumes: doll costume patterns, doll magazines, presentation sewing boxes containing little dolls with their patterns, fabric and sewing supplies, and even child-size sewing machines.

Today one can occasionally find, from the attic, examples of this child-sewing. In one poignant example recently sold at auction, a 1915 S.F.B.J. French doll came with a hand-sewn wardrobe of about 30 items. There were two examples of each article of clothing: one meticulously sewn and embroidered by mother, the other simplistically pieced together by daughter's learning hand.

Thus, side-by-side in the world of dolls, two categories of costumes have existed for a century and a half: the commercially-made and the family-made. And within each category are different levels. Commercial doll costumes can range from couturier models to mass produced garb. Family-made can range from great-aunt's superb handworkmanship to the young child's naive attempts.

As the collecting of antique doll costumes becomes more widespread, collectors are confronted with these historical side-by-side worlds. This makes the study of authenticity and chronology somewhat difficult. To complicate the matter even further, today's collector must take into account costumes "made in the manner". Do not assume that this necessarily means that the costume was made only last year or the year before. A fashion gown "in the manner of" 1865, for example, may have been in 1885 to replace a worn out example! In another recent auction example, a group of Neapolitan figures from the early 19th century were wearing costumes representing Shakespearean actors of the 17th century; these costumes had actually been made in the early 20th century to replace the original Neapolitan costumes!

In this confusing world what's a collector to do? Clearly, study and exposure are the answers. Initially, study through books, fashion journals, and historical documents is invaluable. One will learn styles that prevailed at a certain time, as well as which fabrics and colors were available and/or popular, and when certain sewing techniques became available. Inconsistencies will become obvious, the more one studies. Carried to a ludicrous extreme, if one were to find a zipper in an 1865 dress, one might well be concerned as to its authenticity! Machine-sewing in a gown presumably of the 1830's would be a certain clue to its actual later production. On the other hand, knowledge can be a positive weapon, as well. Collectors finding nylon in a dress of the late 1920's might be concerned that the dress was "wrong", assuming that nylon only appeared later; that could be misfortune! Corduroy, also, seems to us a "modern" fabric, yet it was popularly used in bebe dresses of the 1880's.

But beyond book learning, nothing can substitute for exposure to the actual objects. Gradually, by touching the fabrics and the construction of those fabrics, by closely examining sewing techniques, one gains a "sense" of the historical rightness of that costume. Collectors are urged, whenever possible, to find opportunities to view and handle authentic examples of historical costumes. (A note of caution: given the fragility and rarity of antique doll costumes, excessive handling is clearly detrimental.) For study purposes, collectors are urged to use, seek out badly-worn costumes or costume fragments, those whose only useful life remaining is as a study object. For the study of costumes that remain in good historical condition, collectors are urged to wear white cotton gloves during inspection. For the preservation of these costumes, collectors are urged to invest in acid-free storage boxes and acid-free tissue papers, and to store these costumes carefully when not in use.

Who Collects Antique Doll Costumes?

Certainly, the largest number of costume collectors are those wishing to dress their dolls. There can be no question that dolls attired in clothing of their specific period have a certain elan that simply cannot be duplicated by reproduction clothing, however accurately styled or authentically sewn the reproduction may be. Many of these collectors, realizing the historical value of the antique clothing, allow their dolls to wear the costumes only on special occasions.

There are a growing number of collectors who simply collect antique doll costumes with no idea of using the costume to dress a doll. They simply want the costume for its own beauty. There is a special nostalgia that attaches itself to a slightly faded, yet still glorious, party dress of the 1880's. A simple doll's homespun nightshift of the 1860's, with meticulous, impossibly small stitches can inspire reverie, respite from today's burly world. Who made this? A child? Her grand-mother? Where did they live? How did they live? This historical connection with the past, inspired by simple objects, is not an emotion to be belittled; it is healthy and sane and important.

Some collectors, also, pursue doll costumes with a goal of assembling a trousseau or wardrobe for a specific doll that they own. This may be a French fashion doll of the 1870's or a classic German dolly-face model, circa 1910, from a firm such as Kestner. Such a project combines the best of two worlds: it allows the collector to "dress" a particular doll, yet in the main, the costume is not exposed, being placed in the doll's trunk or armoire along with her other garments.

Today's doll couturiers also collect antique doll costumes for their obvious value in first-hand study of construction details.

The growing study of historical "real people" fashion has also prompted collecting of antique doll costumes. These miniature examples are often identical in every detail to their larger counterparts, and are, decidedly, easier to store and handle.

Concerning the Costumes Shown Herein

The costumes in this book have been subjected to rigorous mental examination concerning their authenticity. Costume and textile experts in both France and America have corroborated in their documentation. Approximate historical dates have been given for each costume, based upon construction and styles. These dates are approximate and may vary by some few years. In a few cases when certainty was not possible the phrase "later couturier made of old fabrics" has been used rather than a "circa" date. Of most difficulty in determining dates are undergarments, nightwear and baby costumes, whose style and construction, as far as dolls were concerned, remained fairly constant throughout much of the second half of the 19th century.

The doll costumes in this book number nearly 500. In light of this, one might well wonder about their rarity. Do not be deceived. Historical doll costumes in good to excellent condition are extraordinarily rare. Each year more are exposed to climatic hazards as well as simple carelessness in handling.
This collection has been many, many years in the making and it is unlikely its scope and quality will be seen again.

Chapter I

Early Fashion Costumes
1830 - 1860

1. Three-Piece Calico and Muslin Ensemble
Comprising printed muslin blouse with extremely-full gigot sleeves, full gathers at top of sleeves, wide collar with hand-stitched detail, string-tie at neckline, strings en coulisse waist back. And brown calico skirt with pleated flat front, cartridge pleated back, brown muslin lining, hook and eye closure. And fine cotton apron with two bellows pockets, hook and eye closure. 6 1/2" shoulder width. 11" waist. 15" skirt length. Circa 1830.

2. Woven Workbasket and Needlepoint Slippers
The open top, open-work woven basket of variegated colors has solid-woven base, designed to carry hand-work. And blue gros-point hand-woven slippers with tiny floral designs, padded interiors, muslin lined, silk edging, leather soles. 5 1/2" W. basket. 3 1/3" L. slippers. Circa 1850.

3. Straw Bibi Bonnet
Tightly-woven narrow bands of straw form a tightly-fitting cap at back of head, a wide 3" brim that hides the face. Fine gauze and silk lining, silk ribbons and streamers, tiny blue flowers and blue silk ribbons trim the inside and out. 2 1/2" back of head width. Circa 1845.

4. Straw Bibi Bonnet
Narrow bands of straw in alternate diamond and slat patterns form the bonnet with tightly-fitting rounded cap at back of head, wide 3" brim with scalloped straw edging that hide the face. Fine gauze lining, ivory silk ribbons and streamers inside and out. 2 1/2" back of head width. Circa 1845.

5. Plaid Calico Gown and Pantalets
Plaid calico cotton gown has set-in lined yoke, cartridge-gathered bodice, 1" set-in waist band, cartridge-gathered skirt, hook and eye and button/loop closures, very full modified-gigot sleeves with pleats at the shoulders, button cuffs, and an unusual ruffle that captures the sleeve's fullness at the upper arm. Self-piping trims the neck, yoke, sleeves, sleeve ruffle and cuffs. With matching pantalets having contrasting calico print torso and matching plaid legs, drawstring waist. 5 1/2" shoulders. 8" waist. 19" overall. 15" L. pants. Circa 1830.

6. Patterned Rose Silk Dress
Of rose silk with woven petal pattern in slightly contrasting color, the dress has fully-lined fitted top with rounded neckline, dropped shoulders, fitted waist, pleated skirt. The very full gigot sleeves are created by gathers at top, bordered by the tiniest cartridge pleats. Self-piping trims the neckline, shoulders, under-arm seams and cuffs, and waist. Hook/eye and button/loop closures. 4 3/4" shoulder width. 8 1/2" waist. 16" overall. Circa 1830.

7. Maroon Silk Dress
A variation of #5, the dress has print-muslin lined yoke and bodice back, pleated bodice with hidden muslin bands to hold the pleats, V-shaped center of bodice, 1" waist-band, very full gigot-sleeves with cartridge pleating at shoulders and pleated muslin-lined skirt. Self-piping at neckline, yoke, and cuffs. 4 1/2" shoulders. 8" waist. 18" overall. Circa 1830.

8. Calico Print Dress with Pantalets and Bavolet Bonnet
Of cream and rose printed calico with tiny floral design, the dress has square-cut neckline with slightly-dropped shoulders, very full gigot sleeves with cartridge pleating at shoulders, fitted cuffs, gathered bodice, 1" set-in waistband, gathered skirt, button/loop closures. With matching pantalets having strings en coulisse waist. And self-lined rose-cotton bonnet with elaborate ruching, ruffled brim and bavolet. 5 1/2" shoulders. 7 1/2" waist. 18" overall length. 16" pants length. Circa 1830.

9. White Homespun Cotton Dress and Pantalets
Of tightly-woven white cotton homespun, with rounded neckline trimmed with piping, long narrow sleeves with wrists having button and loop closure, shoulder piping, dart-shaped bodice, shaped waist above tight cartridge pleats, full skirt, button back. With cotton pantalets having tucks and cutwork trim. 5" shoulder width. 6" waist. 13" overall length. Circa 1840.

10. Silk Bibi Bonnet and Woven Reticule
Of bronze-green silk the bonnet has gathered back with stiffened gauze lining for shape, very wide stiffened brim with ivory silk lining, ruffled bavolet. The woven silk purse (reticule) has alternate bands of dark mauve and ecru with tassel trim and drawstrings. 2 1/2" back of bonnet. 1" L. purse. Circa 1845.

11. Wooden-handled Silk Fan
The fan is of stiffened ivory silk with hand-painted decorations, with border of gold braid, gold metallic decorations, wooden handle, silk tassels. 7" overall length. Early 19th century.

12. Bone-handled Arched Silk Fan
The arch-shaped fan is of stiffened ivory silk and is decorated with flowers in rose, yellow and blue above a wide blue band. Applied gilt ormulu decorations add richness. The bone handle is decorated also. 5" overall length. Early 19th century.

13. Bone-handled Rounded Silk Fan
The round-shaped fan of stiffened ivory silk is decorated with daisies, leaves, roses and gilt ormulu decorations to abstractly suggest birds and bees, bone-handle. 6" overall length. Early 19th century.

14. Bone-handled Diamond-Shaped Silk Fan
The diamond-shaped fan of stiffened ivory silk is decorated with blue lattice design under roses and vines, and decorated with gilt ormulu. Gilt ormulu also trims the bone handle. 5" overall length. Early 19th century.

15. Bone-handled Cloche-shaped Silk Fan
The cloche-shaped fan of stiffened ivory silk is decorated with blue petals and roses, has a lattice-decorated border and applique gilt ormulu decorations, bone handle. 4 1/2" L. Early 19th century.

16. Woven Metallic Silk Purse in Presentation Box
Rich mauve/purple/black and green woven circular design is heightened with metallic threads, has scalloped border, gilt metal clasp and handle, and original presentation box. 2 1/2" diameter. Mid-19th century.

17. Black and Gold Silk Woven Reticule
Bronze-gold and black silk threads woven in an intricate Moorish design, with openwork top, tassel trim, drawstrings. 3" L. Mid-19th century.

18. Purple Silk Woven Reticule in Presentation Box
In similar pattern to #16, the reticule has open-work scalloped drawstring top, three-tassel trim, is contained in matching presentation box. 3" L. bag. Mid-19th century.

19. Teal Blue and Brown Silk Woven Reticule
Soft teal blue bands contrast with earth-tone brown bands with shadow design. The bag is decorated with zig-zag scalloped teal blue bands, has drawstring top, matching fringed trim. 4" L. bag. Mid-19th century.

20. Emerald Green and Gold Silk Woven Reticule
Of green silk threads with woven gold pattern, the reticule has drawstring top, fringed and tasseled trim. 2 1/2" L. bag. Mid-19th century.

21. Blue Silk Woven Reticule
Of midnight-blue silk woven threads with intertwined tapestry pattern flowers and ivory bands, drawstring top with three-color woven border, blue fringed tassel. 3 1/2" L. bag. Mid-19th century.

22. Apple Green Silk Woven Reticule in Labelled Box
Of apple green silk woven threads with bands of darker green and rose petals, two color-woven drawstring top, three color fringed tassel. Contained in original box labelled F. Marquis/44 rue Vivienne/69 passage des Panoramas/Paris. 2 1/2" L. bag. Mid-19th century.

23A. Blue and Cream Flannel Bonnet
Of lightweight wool flannel in narrow blue and cream stripes the wire-framed bonnet has gathered back with three rows of tight gathers, double row of gathers at sides of head with scalloped edging, wide brim and bavolet with second inside layer of cream flannel, each layer edged with scalloped diamond-points, muslin lining, silk ribbons and streamers. To fit 5 1/2" head width. Circa 1860.

22A. Printed Muslin Frock and Undergarments
Of fine white muslin printed with delicate sprigs of tiny red flowers, the high-waisted gown has delicate strings en coulisse at rounded neckline and cuffs of short puffed sleeves, double strings en coulisse at high waist, tiny cartridge pleats at shoulders. And matching undergarments comprising simple chemise with one-button back and pantalets with open back, drawstring set-in waistband. 3 1/2" shoulders. 7" undergarment waist. 15" overall gown. Circa 1830.

23. Four White Cotton Garments
(1). Sturdy homespun nightshirt with set-in V-shaped panels at sides, very delicate cutwork and edging, roll-up sleeves, 6" shoulders. (2). Apron with pin-bib, 1" set-in waistband, ties, cartridge pleating, 2 large pockets, 12" skirt length. (3). Pantalets with open-back, set-in waist band with ties, narrow legs, narrow border of lace, 7 1/2" waist. (4). Sturdy homespun nightshirt with edging at V-cuts on shoulders, side-flared sides, 6" shoulder width. Circa 1840.

24. Fine Muslin Print Dress with Fitted Bodice
Of fine muslin in tiny rose and white checkered pattern, the dress has Sevigne bodice which tapers to a tight-fitting waist with diamond-point stomacher shaped by a single 1 1/2" midriff vertical bone, (the unusual shaping allowing generous fullness to the bosom), 3/4 bodice lining, self-piping at neckline, cuffs, shoulders, center yoke and waist, long narrow sleeves with band of self-ruching trim at upper arms, button cuffs with lace trim, very full skirt with cartridge pleating, hook and eye closure, strings en coulisse at neckline. 7 1/2" shoulders. 10 1/2" waist. 20" overall length. Circa 1840.

25. A Matching Muslin Dress
Of identical size, pattern and style to the preceding. Circa 1840.

26. Floral Design Woven Reticule
Shaded pink-to-red roses and buds are woven onto a black background, and enclosed by six various borders, drawstring top and multi-color tassels to complement the purse colors. 5 1/2" body. Circa 1840.

**27. Plum and Gold
Silk Woven Miser Purse**
Of loosely-woven plum and gold metallic silk threads, the purse is designed to drape over a waist-sash; matching thread-covered bands at center, matching elaborate tassels and fringe. 10" extended length excluding fringe. Circa 1840.

**28. Royal Blue and
Gold Silk Woven Miser Purse**
Alternate bands of royal blue and metallic gold are woven in different patterns, separated by delicate lace bands, a single ring captures the purse opening and forms gathers for the purse to drape over a waistband; trimmed with elaborate matching fringe and tassels. 12" extended length excluding fringe. Circa 1840.

**29. Zig-zag Pattern
Woven Wool Reticule**
Hand-woven reticule in rich zig-zag pattern of black, maroon, gold and green has unusual pleated shaping, draw-strings of matching threads trimmed with matching balls, tassels and fringe, cotton sateen lining. 4" body. Circa 1840.

30. Sheer Muslin Blue Flowered Dress
Of very fine sheer white muslin printed with tiny blue pin-dots and flowers, the high-waist dress has fitted bodice with hidden cartridge pleats at center allowing slight fullness, low rounded neckline with hand-made trim, elbow-length sleeves with lace edging, fitted waistband with button closure, cartridge-pleated full skirt with one row of tucking. 2 1/2" shoulder width. 4" waist. 7" overall length. Circa 1840.

31. White Homespun Three-Piece Baby Ensemble
Of white homespun woven into tiniest narrow bands, the ensemble comprises entirely hand-stitched baby gown having full-length front panel trimmed with hand-made rick-rack, long set-in sleeves with turn-up cuffs and lace edging. And full-length cape with gathers below the set-in yoke, Pilgrim collar with feather-stitching, gathered adjustable hood. And short dart-shaped hooded cape with simple soutache. With muslin chemise. 3" shoulder width. 10" overall. Circa 1850.

Chapter II

Early Child Doll Dresses
1860 - 1875

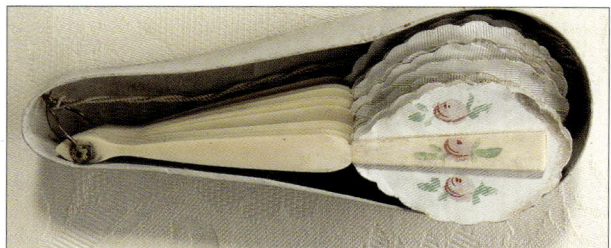

34. Striped Silk Parasol
With painted metal handle and bone hand-grip, the eight-prong parasol forms a rounded shape when opened, is covered with original striped brown/cream silk with floral pattern, long silk fringe. 18" L. Circa 1860.

35. Ivory-Handled Miniature Fan
Thirteen-blade folding ivory handle has fretwork carving, brass belt loop, heart-shaped silk twill panels with brass beads and hand-painted floral designs. 3" L. Circa 1860.

36. Cream/Aubergine Print Grenadine Dress
Of very delicate cream grenadine printed with abstract aubergine designs, the dress has low rounded neckline with tiniest cartridge pleats held by self-banding, generously-full bodice, 1 1/3" set-in waistband, cartridge-pleated full skirt with two 1" rows of tucking, short pagoda sleeves trimmed with double row of furbelows. 8 1/2" shoulders. 18" waist. 22" overall. Circa 1860.

37. Cream/Mauve Patterned Calico Dress
Of cream muslin patterned with tiniest mauve floral pattern and having contrasting bands of leaf-patterned trim, the dress has square-cut low neckline with self-banding and strings en coulisse fastening, generously-full high-waisted bodice, 1" width set-in waistband with hook and eye closure, mancheron sleeves with overlapping rounded panels at shoulders allowing for vigorous child activity. 8 1/2" shoulder width. 18" waist. 20" overall length. Circa 1860.

38. White Cotton Dimity Dress with Cutwork and Tucks
Of fine white cotton dimity, the dress has lace ruffle at low-rounded drawstring neckline, high-waisted bodice with V-shaped empiecement of embroidered cutwork and lace bands framed by narrow bretelles, 1" ruffled mancheron sleeves, strings en coulisse waist, cartridge-pleated skirt with set-in front panel of alternating tucks, cutwork, and lace. 8 1/2" shoulders. 18" waist. 19" overall length. Circa 1865.

32. Printed Calico Two-Piece Dress with Flounced Skirt
The cream muslin, printed with tiniest red and plum flowers, forms a two-piece dress, the blouse having fitted bodice with V-shaped empiecement, bretelles that extend into a wide collar at the back, pagoda sleeves with deep furbelows at the ends, and 3" ruffled peplum over the cartridge-pleated very full skirt; the skirt has three 3 1/2" flounces that extend completely around, and two hidden muslin deep pockets. The costume is trimmed with very narrow cream torsade that defines the shaping. With 3/4 length bodice lining, hook and eye closure, drawstrings at neckline. 10" shoulders. 18" waist. 16" skirt length. Circa 1860.

33. Folding Fan in Original Box
Seventeen-blade ivory or bone folding fan has unusual oval-shaped, scalloped-edged heavy twill-silk-paper blades, the outer blade with delicately painted flowers, silk tassel. Original heavy paper box in specific shape to accommodate the fan. 5" L. Circa 1865.

39. White Cotton Muslin Long-Sleeved Dress
Of fine quality white cotton muslin, the dress has low-rounded neckline with narrowest self-piping, fully-lined bodice with generously gathered center-front empiecement and form-fitting sides and back, set-in high waistband, full gathered skirt, coat sleeves with narrow band of lace at cuffs, self-piping at shoulders and armbands, hook and eye closures. 9" shoulders. 19" waist. 22" overall. Circa 1860.

40. White Cotton Pique Pouf Sleeve Dress with Soutache Trim
Of horizontally-banded white cotton pique, the very-high-waisted dress has snug-fitting bodice, rounded collar with narrow self-piping, box-pleated full skirt, pouf sleeves whose fullness is achieved by box pleats at shoulders, turn-up graduated-width cuffs, piping at shoulders, rich soutache design on bodice and skirt, button and loop closure. 5 1/2" shoulder width. 11" midriff. 14" overall. Circa 1860.

41. Sheer Tulle Blouse
Of delicately-woven tulle, the rounded-neck blouse has ruffled tulle fraise and cuffs bordered by narrow band of heavier lace, vertical rows of tucking on front and back bodice and on 3/4" length sleeves, strings en coulisse waistband, 2" peplum, button and loop closure. 9" shoulder width. Circa 1860.

42. White Cotton Dimity Blouse
Of fine white cotton dimity, the blouse has rounded neckline with narrow neckband of lace, four rows of shirring at each shoulder, graduated shirring at center waistband allowing generously-full bodice, set-in waistband, 1 1/2" peplum with scalloped edging, elbow-length trumpet sleeves with matching scalloped edging, hook and eye and button closures. 9" shoulders. 13" waist. Circa 1860.

43. Woven Straw Bourrelet or Puddin' Cap
The circular tightly-woven round cap, designed to perch atop the head, has loosely-woven straw crest, ribbon trim. The cap was designed for young children learning to walk, as a protection against harm to the head when falling. 5" diameter at inside rim. Circa 1860.

44. Woven Straw Bourrelet or Puddin' Cap
Oval-shaped tightly-woven "walking" cap has blue silk bound edging and trim, gauze net lining. 5" diameter at inside rim. Circa 1860.

45. White Cotton Nainsook Dress and Silk Bonnet
Of white cotton nainsook, the dress has bodice with square-shaped neckline and V-shaped empiecement constructed of alternate bands of narrow tucks and entredeux embroidery. A scalloped-edge trim edges the empiecement and extends down the entire length of dress, and edges the neckline and puffed sleeves, as well. There are four rows of tucks around the hemline of the sweep-length skirt, button closure. And silk bavolet bonnet with overall ruching, ruffled brim and crown, embroidered inset at back, silk ties. 4" shoulders. 7 1/2" waist. 12 overall length. Circa 1865.

46. White Cotton Pique Long Gown
Of narrow-ribbed white cotton pique, the high-waisted robe has flat-cut flared front panel bordered by wide box pleats at sides and back that are drawn together with strings en coulisse at back waist, mancheron sleeves with braid and embroidery, embroidery-edged collar, pearl buttons at neck, 2" W. scalloped cut-work bretelles extend the entire front of robe, enclosing seven alternate bands of braid and soutache. Six rows of tucking extend around the bottom of skirt. 6 1/2" shoulder width. 16" loose high waist. 22" overall length. Circa 1870.

47. Four-Piece Ensemble

Comprising white cotton Marseilles flannel-lined princess-style robe with square-cut neckline, mancheron sleeves, set-in back bodice and waist, box-pleated back skirt, elaborate overall soutache trim. And white cotton pique jacket with dart-shaped back centered by box-pleated tail, mancheron sleeves, pleated edging and soutache trim overall. And full-length white cotton pique cape with fern-pattern braid trim and 2" L. of broderie Anglaise. And tulle bonnet with double row of wire-framed brim which give shape to extravagant gathers at front, decorated with ivory silk ribbon clusters and silk streamers. 6 1/2" shoulders. 16" loose high waist. 18" overall length. Circa 1870.

48. Indigo Blue Silk Surah Frock
Of rich indigo blue silk surah with narrow twill pattern, the high-waisted dress has square-cut neckline, bretelle-edged bodice centering a soutache-decorated empiecement, lantern sleeves with box-pleats at shoulders and cuffs, gathered skirt, black silk binding at neckline, cuffs, and bretelle edges, rich black soutache on bretelles, skirt and yoke, muslin-lined bodice, button/loop closure. 7" shoulder width. 14" waist. 16" overall. Circa 1860.

49. Black Leather Shoes with Blue Silk Trim
Hand-stitched shoemaker's black leather shoes with square toes, half-muslin lining, blue silk edging on tops and ankle straps, blue silk rosettes with silver buckles, soft tan kid-leather tacked-on soles. 4 1/2" L. 1 1/2" W. Circa 1860.

50. Woven Straw Bourrelet or Puddin' Cap in Original Box
The oval-shaped tightly-woven firm-sided "walking" cap has blue velvet edging and decoration, gauze net lining, and is contained in its original box labelled "Maison de Blanc/ Trousseaux/Layettes/Costumes d'Enfants/ Dupas-Pons. 7 rue de la loge/Montpellier." 5 1/2" diameter inside width. Circa 1860.

51. Silk Taffeta Blue Plaid Dress
Of very crisp silk taffeta in blue/green/gold plaid, the dress has rounded high neckline, dart-shaped form-fitted bodice, gored flat-front skirt with constructed pleats at skirt sides and back, vandyked hem, coat sleeves with gusset at back sleeve for easier movement, black velvet edging at neckline, cuffs, and skirt, grelot edging of yoke. Brown cotton-sateen-lined bodice, hook and eye closure. 8" shoulders. 11 1/2" waist. 21" overall length. Circa 1855.

52. Black Velvet Bolero Jacket and Red Silk Leggings
The black velvet bolero jacket has long sleeves with dart-shaping at back elbows, red silk lining, brass bells trimming the entire outer edges. With muslin-lined red silk gaiters, having gold braid trim, leather footstraps, 12 brass buttons/buttonholes. 9" shoulder width. 10" mid-calf diameter. Circa 1860.

53. Collection of Four Purses
Comprising gold and black woven miser purse with silver bead trim, 7" extended length; blue and cream woven double-hung purse with silver clasp and woven silver bead trim, marked "Depose Paris"; and two similar cream silk woven miser purses with silver beads and gold ring, 6" extended length. Circa 1850.

54. Three-Piece Baby Ensemble
Comprising cream silk satin douillette with gathers below the fitted yoke, pleated full sleeves with banded cuffs, 8" capelet collar with lace trim and ruching, matching lace trim on coat, full-muslin lining. And fine muslin gown with empiecement of alternating bands of lace and gathers edged with beading lace and silk ribbons, having full gathers at back, long lace-trimmed sleeves. And muslin chemise with draw-string neckline, button front, cotton lace edging. 4 1/2" shoulder width. 16" overall length of coat. Circa 1865.

55. White Jaconet Baby Gown and Walking Cap
Fine white sheer jaconet gown with fitted bodice, set-in waistband, full-length flat front panel edged by curved self-fabric tablier ruffles, gathered back, button/loop closures, 3/4 length coat sleeves, narrow border of lace trim and blue silk ribbons. With woven straw bourrelet or puddin' cap edged in braided pale blue and cream velvet ribbons. 4" shoulders. 16" overall. Circa 1860.

56. White Fine Muslin Baby Gown
Of very delicate muslin, the gown has square-cut neckline, princess-shaped front centered by vertical bands of flat lace, ruffled lace and cutwork, and bordered by full-length bretelles that extend over the shoulders to the back waist, framing gathers at the center back waist. There are three rows of ruffles at hemline, " and 3/4 length sleeves with lace edging. Hook and eye closures. 1 3/4" shoulders. 11" waist. Circa 1860.

57. White Dimity Baby Gown and Full Slip
Of very delicate white dimity, the high-waisted gown has fitted bodice with yoke of guipure lace edged by lace bretelles, rounded neckline and short lantern sleeves with lace edging, feather-stitched waistband, extended length cartridge-pleated skirt with strings en coulisse waist, graduated-width front skirt panel with rows of tucking alternating with 11 rows of guipure lace and bordered by ruffled Valenciennes lace. With matching cotton slip having strings en coulisse waist. 3" shoulders. 6 1/2" waist. 21" overall. Circa 1865.

58. White Marseilles Cotton Baby Gown
Of waffle-weave flannel-lined Marseilles cotton, the gown has high waist, full-length flat-front panel of graduated width decorated with broderie Anglaise, braid and elaborate soutache clusters, set-in back bodice, box-pleated back skirt, self-belt, button closure, 3/4 length curved sleeves with cutwork and braid trim. 5" shoulders. 12" loose high waist. 19" overall length. Circa 1860.

59. Seven-Piece Baby Ensemble
Comprising white cotton high-waisted gown with square-cut neck and 3/4 length sleeves both edged in torchon lace, box-pleated long skirt with long ties edged in torchon lace, flannel lining, button/loop closure. And similarly-cut untrimmed gown with mancheron sleeves and strings en coulisse neckline. And flannel-lined matelasse jacket. And two different dainty cotton jackets. And lace-edged cotton cutwork bonnet. And pillowed bunting with scalloped-edge cutwork. 4 1/2" shoulder width. 10 1/2" high waist. 16" overall length. Circa 1865.

59A. Six-Piece Matching Baby Ensemble
A matched and identically-sized set with #59 except lacking high-waisted gown. Circa 1865.

60. Five-Piece Baby Ensemble
Comprising white muslin shift with set-in yoke and gathered front, curved sleeves and lace edging; another muslin shift with flared sides, flat button front, lace edging; jacquard weave jacket with rolled collar; pique bib-collar with drawstring tie waist, button neck, cutwork edging; and lace-edged cotton cover. 3 1/2" shoulder width. 11" shift length. Circa 1860.

61. Two Sets, Marseilles Cotton Douillette and Cap
The matched sets, of white waffle-weave Marseilles cotton, comprise coat with set-in fully-lined yoke, box pleats, 3/4 length sleeves with white cutwork cuffs, piping at yoke and shoulders, 12" L. attached flared cape with cutwork trim at edge and matching cutwork collar. And matching caps with flannel lining, drawstrings and long ties. 7" shoulder width. 21" overall length. Circa 1865.

62. Three-Piece Baby Ensemble
Comprising jacquard weave flannel-lined jumper with high-waist fitted bodice, flat-front skirt, gathered back skirt, diamond-edged cotton trim. And white Marseilles cotton coat with flannel-backing, set-in bodice and long sleeves, box pleats, hip-length flared cape collar with cutwork edging. And cotton batiste cap with seven tiers of ruche, double ruffled edge and drawstrings for fit. 4" shoulder width. 15" coat length. Circa 1865.

Chapter III

The Classic Fashion Doll
1855-1875

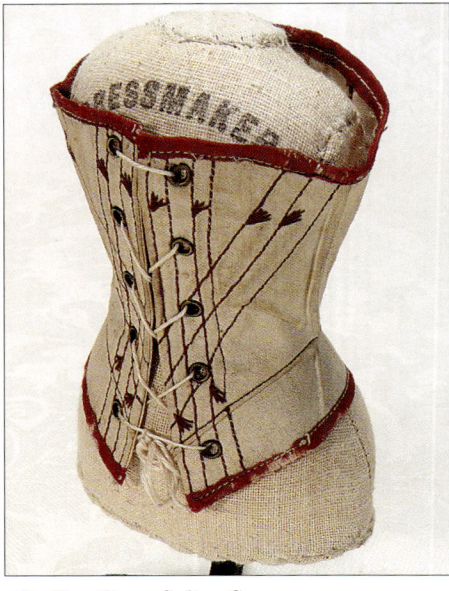

63. Two-Piece Calico Gown with Matching Crinoline and Corset
Of white calico printed with abstract pattern in shades of rose, the two-piece gown comprises basque with dropped shoulders trimmed with piping, narrow sleeves with double row of furbelows at cuffs lending a trumpet-like effect, fitted waistband with cluster of cartridge pleats at center front and back, gathered peplum, detachable decorative waist bow; and cartridge pleated white muslin skirt with two rows of gathered calico ruffles. With original coutil boned corset and five-ring wire-framed crinoline with cotton casing. 5" shoulder. 7" waist. 9" skirt length. Circa 1855.

64. Three Cotton Night Gowns
Comprising white ribbed muslin gown with lace-edged placket front, gathers at back collar for fullness, long sleeves with lace edging, lace stand-up collar. And white muslin with faux-placket front defined by nine rows of nun's tucks and featherstitching and blue-thread scalloped edging, matching blue scalloped edge on cuffs of long sleeves and ruffled collar, set-in back yoke with button closure; and white muslin gown with set-in yoke above gathered gown, placket front with tatted edging, long sleeves, tatting at cuffs and neckline. Each 4 1/2" shoulder width. About 14" length. Circa 1865.

65. Eleven Fashion Doll Undergarments and Accessories
Comprising printed muslin jacket with handmade rick-rack trim, muslin chemisette with button and loop closure, scalloped edge drawnwork edging; homespun chemisette with handmade rick-rack shoulder cuffs and collar edging; pantalets with box-pleated edging and tucks, set-in waist; pantalets with set-in waist, full legs, fitted leg cuffs with ruffled edging; muslin jacket with pagoda sleeves, red scalloped edging; percale jacket with flared sides, sleeve piping trim; pique bib-collarette with double lappet front centered by set-in panel, decorated with generous banding and lace edging; two pairs of cotton knit stockings (one woven to shape, one hand-stitched), and lace-edged handkerchief. 4 1/2" shoulder width. Circa 1865.

66. Pair of Printed Muslin Night Gowns
Each is of fine sheer muslin, one printed in blue floral pattern, the other with roses and trailing ribbons; each with placket front centering five rows of nun's tucks, set-in yoke at back above full gathers, long sleeves with unusual extended length cuffs, set-in collars, hand-made cotton lace at collar and cuffs. 5" shoulder width. 16" length. Circa 1870.

67. Pale-Blue Silk Mousseline Child Fashion Gown
Of pale blue silk mousseline with most delicate shadow weave, the gown has square-cut neckline with mancheron sleeves hidden under wide bretelles which extend into back collar, set-in V-shaped bodice edged by self-piping, set-in waist from which extends castellated trim onto the gathered skirt, hook and eye closure. The gown is trimmed with contrasting shadow-plaid silk with fringed edging at bodice, collars, castellations and sleeves. With white cotton petticoat with set-in V-shaped waistband. 4" shoulders. 7" waist. 13" overall length. Circa 1860.

68. Blue Silk Fringed Parasol
Of blue striped silk, the parasol has long blue/cream silk fringe, brass handle, ivory tips, eight prongs. 9" overall length. Circa 1865.

69. Stiffened Muslin Capote Bonnet
The stiffened muslin capote bonnet encloses the sides and back of head, tying at the throat, shaped by large pleats at the lower back, trimmed by bands of pleats and ribbon-insertion lace around the face, lace and silk bow trim, grosgrain ribbon trim. About 2" width. Circa 1865.

70. Black Leather Shoes with Blue Silk Ribbons
Of soft black leather the shoes are banded in brown silk, have straps which tie with blue silk ribbons at the top of the foot appearing as simply part of the slip-in shoe, gold buckles with blue silk bows, brown soft kid soles. 2 1/4" L. Circa 1860.

71. Black Leather Shoes with Blue Silk Banding
Black leather slip-on shoes have muslin lining, blue silk banding, silver buckles with blue silk bows, brown soft kid soles. 1 3/4" L. Circa 1860.

72. Black Leather Shoes with Black Bows
Black leather slip-on shoes have black slip banding, black silk bows with gold buckles, hand-stitched brown soft kid soles. 2" L. Circa 1860.

73. Bengaline Silk Three-Piece Gown and White Batiste Blouse
The gown comprises bodice of muslin-lined grey bengaline silk with blue silk banding, hook and eye closure; with blue silk taffeta skirt with flat-front and cartridge-pleated sides and back; and

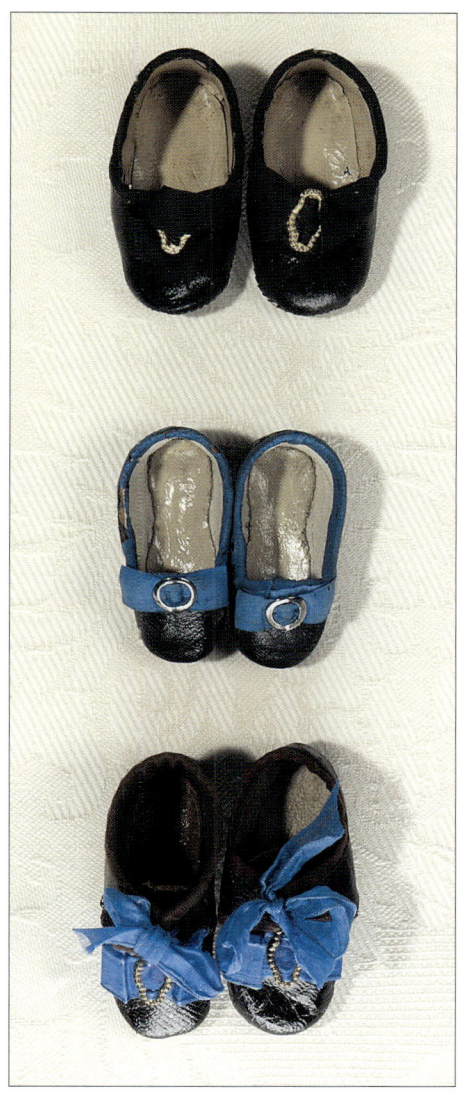

grey bengaline silk polonaise with flat-front, flounce back, and modified pannier sides achieved by horizontal gathers at either side of front panel (the gathers covered by blue silk tie-back ribbons that extend, hidden, inside the waistband to support the back flounce), muslin waistband, hook and eye closure. And white nainsook blouse with tucked front, button back, broderie Anglaise and border lace at collar and cuffs. 4 1/2" shoulder width. 7 1/2" waist. 8 1/2" skirt waist. Circa 1860.

74. Ivory Silk Faille Capeline
Of ivory silk faille with full muslin lining, the flared-side capeline has blue silk banding at all edges, blue silk bow, and gathered-edge hood with blue banding, the hood stitch-attached to the back of the cape. 4 1/2" shoulder width. 7" L. Circa 1865.

75. *White Cotton Pique Gown with Soutache Trim*
Of horizontally ribbed white cotton pique, the slightly-high-waisted gown has rounded neckline, set-in short sleeves, fitted bodice, gored skirt with darts and gathers, braid edging at collar and cuffs, elaborate white soutache trim on bodice, sleeves, hemline and front panel of skirt. 4" shoulders. 8 1/2" waist. 13" overall length. Circa 1860.

76. *White Cotton Pique Sweep-Length Gown*
Of horizontally ribbed white cotton pique, the gown has high waist defined by gore-shaped panels at front, set-in high yoke at back and interior hidden waistline cord that "pulls" the dress shape together; lace-edged square neckline, mancheron sleeves with 1" border of open-weave lozenge-shaped lace, box-pleats at back that extend from yoke to sweep-length hem, elaborate soutache trim on sleeves, front panel and hemline. 4 1/2" shoulder width. 13" overall length. Circa 1868.

77. *White Cotton Dimity Day Gown*
Of white cotton dimity, the gown has slightly-high-waist, flared-side front achieved by three gore-shaped panels which are defined by ruffled broderie Anglaise; the bottom of center panel having alternate bands of insertion and ruffled broderie Anglaise and braid trim. Low rounded neckline with cotton lace trim, full long-sleeves with cutwork edging and drawstring cuffs, set-in back bodice with gathered sweep-length skirt, button closure. 4 1/2" shoulder width. 16" front length. Circa 1868.

78. *White Printed Cotton Dress*
Of white cotton printed with delicate blue and red abstract floral design the dress has low rounded neckline whose sides evolve into the fully-gathered sleeve tops; short puffed sleeves cartridge-gathered into tight cotton lace bands, generously-gathered bodice, set-in fitted waistband, cartridge-pleated skirt. 5 1/2" shoulders. 9" waist. 15 1/2" overall length. Circa 1860.

79. Blue Printed Muslin Dress with Pagoda Sleeves
Of white muslin with indigo-blue-printed flowers and leaves, the dress has square-cut neckline, set-in generously gathered bodice with self banded neckline, set-in waistband, flare-shaped 3/4 length sleeves with wide double furbelows. full gathered skirt with double row of 3" furbelows. Button and hook/closure. 4 1/2" shoulder width. 8" waist. 12" overall length. Circa 1860.

80. Sheer White Cotton Voile Gown and Matching Cap
Sheer white cotton voile, the gown has low rounded neckline, lantern sleeves generously gathered at the top, set-in waistband, gathered front bodice, fitted back bodice, cartridge-pleated skirt with rows of tucking. Beading lace at neckline, cuffs, waist and hem is interwoven with blue silk ribbons and bows. With matching silk and tulle cap, decorated with interwoven blue silk ribbons. 4 1/2" shoulder width. 9" waist. 13" overall length. Circa 1860.

81. White Printed Muslin Dress with Unusual Sleeves
Of fine white cotton muslin printed with abstract mauve pattern, the dress has high rounded neckline edged with self-piping and lace, muslin-lined front and back yoke, pleated bodice, set-in waistband, gathered skirt, button and hook and eye closure. Unusual sleeves whose upper half is puffed (with form-fitting lining for shape), and bottom half is trumpet-shaped. 4 1/2" shoulder width. 7" waist. 13" overall length. Circa 1860.

82. White Nainsook Cotton Dress with Lantern Sleeve
Of fine white nainsook cotton with low rounded neckline having strings en coulisse fitting, set-in lantern sleeve with banded cuffs and piping trim, gathers at center back and front bodice, set-in waistband, cartridge-pleated skirt. 4 1/2" shoulder width. 7" waist. 13" overall length. Circa 1865.

83. Flowered Calico Gown with Smocked Bodice
Of cream calico with multi-colored floral print, the gown has fully-lined bodice with V-shaped smocked empiecement flanked by graduated-width bretelles and trimmed with lace; smocking at back bodice, fully-lined muslin lantern sleeves with banded cuffs, set-in waistband, fully-lined muslin skirt with attached polonaise, lace and ruffle skirt trim, hook and loop closure. 4 1/2" shoulder width. 7" waist. 13" overall length. 1860 style, possibly later construction.

84. Three-Piece Tarlatan Gown
Of cream tarlatan with interwoven lavender pencil stripes, the costume comprises flared-cut basque with overlapping cut flaps at sides and back, inset 3/4 pagoda sleeves. And 2-panel flounce-shaped skirt with furbelow border. And gathered polonaise with flounce back, drawn-up sides, self-ruffle and bows. Each piece trimmed with narrow purple braid. 2 1/2" shoulder width. 4 1/2" waist. Circa 1860.

85. Brown Leather Sac du Voyage
Of patterned brown leather with tooling decorations, the two-compartment valise has V-shaped soft-sided top with accordion sides, metal frame, twill cord handle, blue paper interior; and firm-sided rectangular base that hinges open separately, with silver-metal clasp, blue paper lining and envelope compartment. 3 1/2" L. Included are pair of brown kid leather gloves. Circa 1865.

86. Ivory-Handled Parasol
With carved ivory handle and tip, the brass-shafted parasol has seven prongs, opens and closes freely, blue silk cover edged by 1 1/2" delicate guipure scalloped-edge lace. 7". Circa 1860.

87. Pair, Tan Kid Leather Shoes with Maker's Mark "J.J."
The slip-on shoes, of soft tan kid leather has scalloped edges, diamond-pointed low vamps, leather soles with incised maker's symbol of a pair of shoes lettered J.J. Band word "trademark", size 8, blue silk bows and star decoration. 2 3/4" L. 1/2" instep. Circa 1860.

88. Fruitwood Patented Valise with Blue Silk Interior
The fruitwood carved valise, designed to resemble kid leather, has details of straps and stitching on exterior, carved handle, brass hinges and interior clasp, blue silk-lined interior with five separate compartments. Gold stamped "patent" on base. 2" W. Circa 1870.

89. Brown Homespun Linen Gown with Polonaise
Of brown homespun linen, the gown has dart-fitted bodice with V-shaped empiecements on front and back bodice that are defined by black velvet banding, five-button front, double-seam curved coat sleeves, gore-shaped skirt with pleats at waist. With separate four-panel flounced polonaise. Furbelow edging on skirt and polonaise, black velvet buttons and banding decoration. 4" shoulder width. 6" waist. 13" overall. Circa 1865.

37

90. Two Brown Linen Pin-Top Tabliers
Of homespun woven linen, each tablier or apron has bodice cover designed to be pinned to dress, set-in waistband with ties, gathered skirt, two pockets. One has white handwork scalloped-edge embroidery around all edges and pockets, small hand-edged handkerchief in pocket. 7 1/2" waists. Circa 1860.

91. Six Pieces Whitewear Cotton Undergarments
Comprising full under-gown with fitted bodice, set-in short sleeves, cartridge-pleated full skirt, button back, simple lace trim; draw-string petticoat with pleated front, V-shaped set-in waistband, sac with stand-up drawn-work collar and cuffs, set-in long sleeves, vertical bands of tucks, embroidery and drawnwork on bodice, button front; chemise with lace-trimmed placket, capelet sleeves and neckline; split drawers with drawstring waist; pantalets with set-in front waist, drawstring back waist. For about 4 1/2" shoulder width. 7" waist. Circa 1865.

92. Tan Leather Shoes Marked J.J. and "Musique" Portfolio
Tan leather ankle shoes with lace front has scalloped edging, applied star-shaped leather decoration in blue and gold, narrow leather soles marked J.J., size 5. And soft kid leather folding portfolio with self-handles, gold-stencilled "Musique", red silk twill lining. 2" L. shoes. 1/3" W. of instep. Circa 1865.

93. Brown Natural Linen Gown and White Blouse
Of light brown natural linen, the gown has fitted shoulders, set-in yoke and waistband which border the gathered front and back bodice, mancheron sleeves with over-lapping panels at shoulders, three box-pleats at front of skirt, double box-pleats around sides and back of skirt, wide tucking band at skirt bottom, decorative black cord trim, hook and eye closures. With white cotton blouse having set-in cuffs, rick-rack edging, drawstring neckline, button back. 4" shoulder. 7" waist. 12" overall. Circa 1860.

94. Brown Silk Twill Heeled Boots with Maker's Mark
Tan silk twill boots with shapely cut to hug the ankle has black leather front panels and covered wooden heels, brown overcast thread edging and six pairs of lacing holes, brown silk laces, rosettes, muslin lining, brown leather soles stamped with shield-shaped insignia. 2 1/3" L. Circa 1865.

95. White Cotton Pique Gown and Basque
Of fine white pique, the gown has tablier-front with wide suspender straps, set-in high waist, double box-pleated skirt, attached flaps at back waist. With matching five-panel basque having shapely waist definition, flared hips, 3/4 length trumpet sleeves. The gown is elaborately decorated with handmade white rick-rack, the jacket with soutache trim. 4" shoulder width. 6" waist. 12" L. overall gown. Circa 1865.

96. Two Leather Purses and "Fables" Book
Two folio-shaped red leather purses with flap fronts have interior accordion-style compartments, gold tooled decorations on exterior, silk cord belt loops. And miniature book of French Fables with illustrations, stories, ivory cover inscribed "Fables", red silk binding and interior covers. 1 1/4" L. book. Circa 1870.

97. Miniature Cranberry Glass Perfume Bottle
Urn-shaped cranberry glass perfume bottle has gilded metal lid with chain handle. 3/4" L. Circa 1870.

98. Ruby Glass Parure
Two sets. One comprising a necklace with ruby glass beads and gilt metal brooch with centered "ruby", and pair of wire-backed matching earrings. Other comprising a necklace of tiny beads alternating with delicate metal links, and pair of matching earrings. Circa 1870.

99. White Pique Gown and Basque with Red Soutache Trim
Of narrow-ribbed white pique, the gown has muslin-lined tablier bodice with wide suspender straps, the back straps extending into oval-shaped flaps that extend 2/3 the length of back skirt, double box-pleated skirt, hook and eye closure. And matching five-panel basque with shapely waist, flared hips, pagoda sleeves. Both pieces trimmed with red edging, three narrow bands of striping, elaborate soutache medallions. 4" shoulder width. 7" waist. 11" overall length. Circa 1865.

100. Red Leather Shoes signed C.C.
Red leather slip-on shoes with little black heels have square-cut vamps, twill lining, red silk interior edging, red silk rosettes with silver button trim, brown leather soles marked "C.C." 2 1/4" L. Circa 1865.

101. Red Leather Shoes signed "J" and Purse
Soft red leather ankle shoes have self-banding, three pairs of lacing holes, silver buckles, brown leather soles signed "J" and size "0". And red leather purse with accordion sides in rose silk twill, silver clasp and belt loops. 1 1/2" L. shoes. Circa 1870.

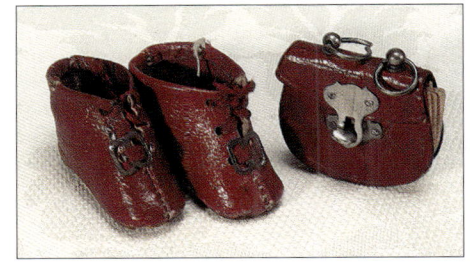

102. Muslin Two-Piece Gown with Undergarments and Cap
Of fine white muslin printed in abstract rose floral pattern, the two-piece gown comprises five panel dart-shaped basque with fitted bodice and waist, flared hips, 3/4 length cotton lining, self-piping at collar and sleeves, pagoda sleeves whose snugly-fitting fully-lined upper sleeves are enhanced by ruching, double row of ruffles at jacket hem, nine hook/eye closures. With three-tiered ruffled skirt with set-in muslin waist. With elaborately constructed dart-shaped handmade boned lacing corset, split drawers with set-in waist, chemisette, and cartridge-pleated white cotton apron with delicate lace edging. And woven straw cap designed to perch atop the head, decorated with rose silk ribbons. 5 1/2" shoulder width. 8" waist. 14" skirt length. Circa 1865.

103. Rose Muslin Two-Piece Gown with Hoop and Seven Undergarments

The rose muslin garment has camargo basque with fitted bodice and elaborately constructed panniers below the hips (of pleats, flounces and pleated back flaps), plastron with gathered cutwork overlay, piping and lace-edged rounded neckline, modified gigot sleeve with cartridge-pleated full upper sleeve, dart-shaped lower sleeve with turn-up cutwork cuff and lace edging, cutwork trim at hem of jacket, rose silk grosgrain ribbons and bows, hook and loop closures. With pleated skirt having additional layer of pleats at back skirt for hoop movement. With matching four-tier muslin-covered crinoline having hook and eye closure on set-in waist; white percale extra blouse with full sleeves, shaped bodice, tie waist, lace trim; pair of batiste cuffed sleeves; two muslin short-sleeved chemisettes; drawstring petticoat with pleated back; and long-sleeved night shift with set-in yoke, full sleeves, embroidered scalloped collar. 5 1/2" shoulder width. 13" jacket length. 9" waist. 9" skirt length. Circa 1865.

104. Horsehair Skirt Shapener
Of very stiff horsehair, the skirt shapener or modified bustle is designed to tie at waist with cotton twill ties, and give shape to the back of the skirt; the sewn-in pleats are held by cotton sateen lining. For about 7" waist. 7" length. Circa 1870.

105. Mauve Silk Padded Corset
The patterned mauve/ivory silk corset is dart-shaped with V-shaped neckline, cotton sateen lining, hook and eye closure, tulle lace at neckline and shoulders. 11" waist. Circa 1860.

106. Fine Muslin Petticoat with Ruffled Train
With flat front, gathered back, set-in waist band with button and loop closure, extended-length back, double row of black-embroidered scalloped and gathered ruffles at hemline. 6 1/2" waist. Circa 1870.

107. Hoop with Train and Two Companion Petticoats
The muslin-covered four-tiered boned hoop has cotton twill ties, and is designed to form shape for gown with train; matching mull and cotton petticoats are shaped with train-style back. 6 1/2" waist. 8" front length. Circa 1870.

108. White Patterned Percale Two-Piece Gown and Undergarments
Of white percale with tiny grey and maroon interwoven design, the two-piece gown comprises five-panel basque with dart-shaped front and back bodice, pagoda-shaped sleeves with gusseted underside, piping at neckline and shoulders, grosgrain banding at jacket front and sleeve edging, ten decorative buttons, hook and eye closure. With cartridge-pleated matching skirt having muslin waistband, set-in hidden muslin pocket with grosgrain edging. And fine muslin petticoat with set-in V-shaped waistband attached by strings en coulisse, tucks, lace. And pantalets with V-shaped set-in waistband, drawstrings. 5 1/2" shoulder width. 16" jacket length. 9" waist. 13" skirt length. Circa 1865.

109. White Blouse, Sacque and Chemisette
Comprising fine muslin sacque with slightly-flared sides, button front decorated with tucks and embroidered-edge placket, double-seam sleeves, embroidered collar; sheer batiste cotton blouse with rounded neckline trimmed with double row of lace, shaped bodice, double-seam long sleeves with double row of lace, four buttons and handmade button holes; and cotton chemisette with double collar, the outer collar with tiny ruffled pleats. About 6" shoulder width. Circa 1860.

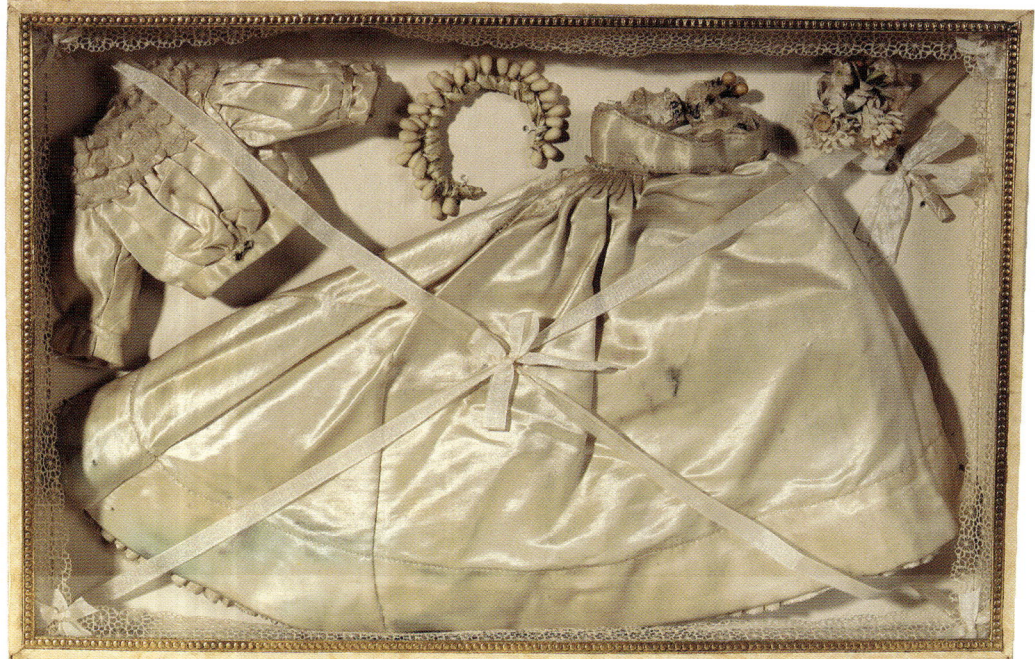

110. Ivory Silk Satin Duchesse Dress and Bonnet
Of fine ivory silk satin duchesse, the dress has dart-shaped fitted bodice with rounded low neckline, slightly-raised waist fitted with interior muslin band, pagoda sleeves, muslin lining, hook and loop closure, box-pleated skirt, self-piping at neckline, waistband and armholes. And matching bavolet bonnet with gathered shaping, net lining, double row of lace ruffles framing the face and interwoven with ivory silk ribbons and streamers. 4 1/2" shoulders. 7" waist. 13" overall length. Circa 1860.

111. Papillote Hair Comb
The tortoiseshell decorative hair comb in butterfly shape is designed to capture a small chignon within its ball-tipped coronet. 1 1/2" base. And handled hair-comb to match signed "Depose". Circa 1870.

***112. Ivory Satin Two-Piece Gown in Presentation Box**
Of ivory silk satin, the two-piece gown has rounded neckline trimmed with ruched tulle, 3/4 length cuffed full sleeves, gathered bodice with set-in waistband, muslin lining. With flat-front sweep-length skirt, having hidden pleat-trim at hemline, set-in waistband. Arranged in glass-window presentation box with gold edging, lace lining, with silk floral anadem and bouquet. 2" shoulders. 4 1/2" waist. 6" front skirt length. Circa 1865.

113. Black Velvet Gown and Figaro Jacket with White Blouse
Black velvet gown has sleeveless fitted bodice with low rounded neckline, seven-panel flared skirt with wide center front panel, decorative black beads and buttons. With matching short flared Figaro jacket having double-seam curved sleeves, silk lining, matching trim. And white dimity blouse with narrow tucks, embroidery, cutwork, button front. 4" shoulder width. 7" waist. Circa 1860.

114. Black Lace Mantle
Of finest black Alencon lace, the full-length cape has constructed shoulders, rolled lace collar, black silk streamers, scalloped black lace at all edges. For about 4 1/2" shoulders. 12" center back fall. Circa 1865.

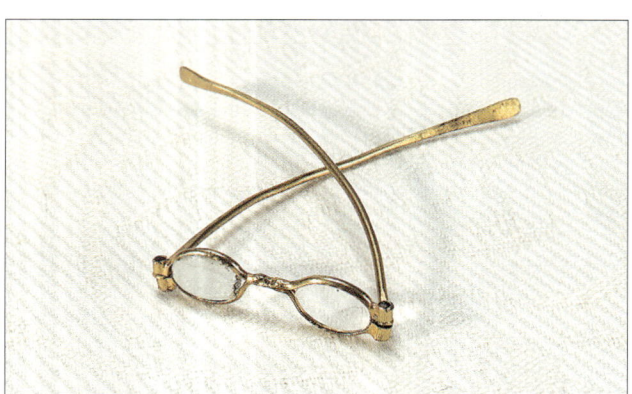

115. Black Velvet Mantelet with Gold Embroidery
Of luxurious black velvet, the four-panel jacket with flared sides has double-seam sleeves, gold silk lining, black braid and black lace edging, lace bretelles at back, tassel drops, overall delicately embroidered "stars" in gold thread. 4 1/2" shoulder width. Circa 1865.

116. Black Silk Evening Gloves
The elbow-length black silk gloves have ties at elbows, separately stitched fingers, set-in thumbs. 5" L. Circa 1870.

117. Gold Dance Card
The gold-framed hinged dance card has richly embossed designs, clasp closure, hinges open to reveal four bone cards, with brooch pin. In old jeweler's box with maker's label. 3/4" L. Circa 1875.

118. Gold Jewelry for Fashion Dolls
The richly gold-plated jewelry includes 5" fold-over decoration for waist, medallion brooch on chain, gold-tipped flexible bracelet, and pair of leaf-shaped drop earrings with pearl "flowers". In early lithographed box labelled "H. Fries/Fabrique de Bijouterie et d'Orfeverie/Berne/Zurich". Circa 1865.

119. Gold Folding Spectacles
The richly gold-plated spectacles have thick glass lenses, hinged sides. 1" lens-to-lens. Circa 1865.

120. Black Silk Taffeta Two-Piece Gown and Blouse
Of black silk taffeta moire, the two-piece gown comprises dart-shaped fitted bodice with square-cut neckline edged in green silk, mancheron sleeves, hook and eye closure. With matching sweep-length skirt with gored flat-front panels and gathered back skirt. With white cotton dimity blouse having tucked bodice and button cuffs, lace edging at collar and cuffs, button and loop back. 4" shoulder width. 7 1/2" waist. 8 1/2" front skirt length. Circa 1868, a nearly-identical pattern was shown in August, 1868, La Poupee Modelle.

121. Black Velvet Paletot with
Green Silk Taffeta Skirt and White Blouse
Of black velvet, the four-panel flared-side jacket has double-seam curved sleeves, hand-embroidered cotton collar, green silk lining, two handmade buttonholes with two silk buttons. With green silk taffeta sweep-length skirt having black windowpane stripe, gore-shape with flat front, gathered back. With white cotton dimity long-sleeved blouse with rounded drop neckline, fitted waist with set-in waistband. 4" shoulders. 7" waist. 8 1/2" front skirt length. Circa 1868.

122. Black Silk Patterned Boots
with Green Trim, and Green Leather Purse
The black silk boots stitched in white quilt pattern have black leather tips, black wooden heels, full muslin lining, ivory braid and green silk pleated trim, six lacing holes, gold buckle, leather soles with Huret-style darker outside rims. With maker's shield-shaped insignia. 2 1/2" l. And pale green leather purse with silk accordion sides, leather straps and waist belt, silk buckle. Circa 1865.

123. Black Velvet Ensemble with Polonaise and Paletot
Black velvet ensemble comprises V-shaped fitted bodice with narrow suspender straps, one-bone construction at center front and back, with attached box-pleated polonaise, trimmed in beaded braid. With matching short paletot having dart-fitted back, pagoda sleeves, black silk banding and black bead braid trim. 4 1/2" shoulder width. 7" waist. Circa 1860.

123A. Black Alencon Lace 'Toilette de Promenade'
Of most delicate black Alencon lace, the square-shaped hair veil is slightly gathered at one corner to form shape for the top of head, is edged with ivory silk ribbons and looped silk self-threads, decorated with two maroon silk bows. 5" square. Circa 1865.

124. Metal-handled Ivory Silk Parasol attributed to Madame LaFarge for Huret
Having narrow metal handle and tip decoratively painted in original yellow with black and red narrow banding, eight short prongs allowing the umbrella to open and close, original ivory silk cover with silk fringed trim. 10" L. Circa 1865.

125. Pale Yellow Silk Taffeta Two-Piece Gown and Undergarments
Of crisp yellow silk taffeta, the intricately constructed dart and tuck-shaped bodice has low square-cut neckline, sleeves constructed as part of bodice with torchon lace shoulder bridges, lace edging at V-shaped back; and full pleated skirt with 2" bands of lace centering the front of skirt and extending around the back hemline. 4" shoulder width. 7" waist. 8" skirt length. 1865 style, possibly later construction.

126. Black Silk Taffeta Two-Piece Gown
Of black silk taffeta, the ensemble comprises fitted bodice with square-cut neckline, suspender straps edged with black velvet and guipure lace, with attached polonaise having flat-front panel, flounced sides and back with hidden construction, black velvet banding and lace trim. With five-tiered ruffled skirt with set-in black muslin waistband, self-piping at edges of ruffles. 3 1/2" shoulder width. 6" waist band. 8 1/2" skirt length. Circa 1860.

127. Black Silk Taffeta Dress
Of crisp black silk taffeta printed with variegated-color polka dots, the one-piece gown has muslin-lined, dart-shaped fitted bodice, high rounded collar, 3/4 length narrow sleeves, self-piping at waist and armholes, pleated skirt with box-pleated front panel, hook and eye closure. Box-pleated bands of black silk with black lace edging trim the neckline, shoulders, sleeves and hem. 3 1/2" shoulder width. 6 1/2" waist. 13" overall length. Circa 1865.

128. Black Silk Taffeta Two-Piece Gown
For miniature doll, the black silk taffeta gown comprises fitted jacket with pagoda sleeves, hook/eye closures; and full skirt with flat-front, gathered back, set-in waistband. Decorative black silk twill ribbons and rick-rack appear on bodice and skirt. 2 1/2" shoulder width. 3" waist. 6" skirt length. Circa 1865.

128A. Pressed Felt Flannel Toque for Fashion Doll
Of grey pressed felt flannel, the toque bonnet has rolled purple velvet brim with matching velvet rosette, mousseline banding and decorations, purple feather and mauve boa, muslin lining. To fit 1 1/2" head width. Circa 1868.

129. Purple Flannel Paletot and Pork-pie Hat
Of purple wool flannel, the three-panel paletot has flared sides, V-shaped neckline, two-seam curved long sleeves, cream/black braid trim, breast pocket, and two cameo buttons. With black pressed-felt hat having flat top, rolled-edge brim with black velvet edging, trimmed with rose/blue fringe and purple silk bows. 4 1/2" shoulder width. Circa 1865.

130. Brown Silk Faille Two-Piece Ensemble
Of brown silk faille, comprising cuirass basque that fits neatly over the hips, dart-shaped back with three box pleats below the waist, V-shaped at bottom of front, two-seam sleeves with faux turn-up cuffs, lighter brown banding at neckline, cuffs and hem, six buttons/button holes, fully lined. With matching skirt having tightly-fitted horizontal pleats at front, modified flounce at back, narrow vertical pleats below the hips, lined, strings en coulisse at back waist to give shape to back flounce. 4" shoulder width. 7" waist. 8" skirt length. Circa 1870.

131. Bone-Handled Black Silk Umbrella
With bone handle and decoratively painted hand-clasp, metal shaft, seven prongs, original black silk cover, opens and closes. 11" length. Circa 1870.

132. Black Leather Chameleon Boots
Black kid leather boots are elaborately cut with four narrow flap bands at either side that are held together by brass buttons and elastic loops, the flaps reinforced by interior silk bands. The cutwork designed to allow stockings to be seen. With black wooden heels, tan leather soles. 2 1/4" length. Circa 1865.

133. Black Leather Laced Boots
Black kid leather with shapely cut, curved tops, the boots have seven pairs of lacing holes, cotton sateen lining, silk banding and narrow ribbon laces, black wooden heels, brown kid soles. Marked "4". 2 1/4" length. Circa 1865.

134. Black Leather Heeled Boots with Brass Buttons and Buckle
Black kid leather boots have wooden black heels, brown silk banding, double rows of brass buttons around which are wound the silk laces, brass buckle with brown silk bows, leather soles. 2 1/2" length. Circa 1865.

135. Black Leather Balmoral Boots Signed M.G.
Black kid leather ankle-high boots have front flap with three button holes and three brass buttons, brown silk banding, black wooden heels. Signed "M.G." and "00". 1 1/2" L. Circa 1870.

136. Brown Wool Flannel Cape and Black Velvet Bonnet
Of brown wool flannel, the flared cape is cut in one continuous piece with 1 1/2" godet at either side of front panel, box-pleat at center back is hidden by V-shaped collar, brown silk banding and tassel trims. With black velvet capote bonnet having rolled brim, set-in back, silk lining, brown silk ribbon trim. 4 1/2" shoulder seam. Circa 1868.

137. Light Brown Flannel Wool Gaiters
Of sturdy brown flannel wool, the gaiters are shape-cut to define the ankles and calves, have brown silk twill banding, silver buttons/button holes, black leather foot straps. 3" ankles circ. 4" length. Circa 1870.

138. Mahogany-Handled Black Silk Umbrella
With nicely carved mahogany wool handle and tip, brass shaft, eight-prongs, (frail) black silk cover with ivory tips, black silk tassel at handle. 8" length. Circa 1870.

139. Dark Green Wool MacFarlane Coat
Of heavy dark green wool the three-panel coat has flared sides, long double-seam sleeves, silk-lined gathered-edge hood, five buttons and button holes. 4 1/2" shoulder width. 13" length. Circa 1868.

140. Light Brown Wool Military-Fit Coat
Of light brown wool, the four-panel coat has slightly flared front, dart-shaped fitted back with two faux-kick-pleats, rolled collar-over-shawl collar, double-seam set-in long sleeves with roll-up cuffs, two pockets, seven buttons/button holes, matching decorative buttons, double rows of decorative over-stitching. 4" shoulder width. 11 1/2" length. Circa 1870.

141. Brown Tweed Flannel Wool Coat
Brown/orange flannel wool tweed coat is cut in four panels with flared sides, wide Pilgrim collar gathered up in the back and held with self-rosette, gathered full sleeves with gathered cuffs, two rounded pockets with gathering at tops, five black silk buttons/button holes. 4 1/2 shoulder width. 12" overall length. Circa 1865.

142. White Fur Pelerine in Original Box
Of plush white fur with head, bead eyes, bared teeth, in original green edged heavy paper box. 9" length. Circa 1870.

143. Navy Blue Wool Camargo Basque
Of rich navy blue wool the basque has long dart-shaped fitted front with 11 brass buttons and button holes, self-cording collar, the sides drawn up into three horizontal pleats decorated with brass buttons, the back with dart-fitting above the waist, and elaborately-constructed bustle achieved by double box pleats and interior ties, long sleeves with wide Pilgrim cuffs. 6" shoulder width. 16" front length. 20" back length. Circa 1870.

144. White Fur Muff with Tails in Original Box
The long-haired white fur muff has tiny head with blue bead eyes, brown tails, padded ivory silk lining, ivory silk ribbons and bows, twill cord, original blue-paper-edged white box. 5" W. Circa 1875.

145. Black Leather Ankle Boots, Size 5
Black leather ankle boots have narrowed toes, flap-over sides with four brass buttons/button holes, shapely-cut ankles, white-overstitching, leather soles, tacked-on wooden heels, marked "5". 3" L. Circa 1875.

146. Brown Leather Flat Shoes
Of soft brown leather with cut-out insteps, ankle straps that attach with white pearl buttons and elastic straps, silver buckle trim, glued-on soles, signed "2". Circa 1865.

147. Cobbler's Cut-work Leather Boots with Thick Soles
High leather boots whose cut-work tops are stitched onto leather lowers have 12 pairs of metal-edged lacing holes, thick leather soles, thicker nailed-on heels. 3 1/2" L. Circa 1865.

148. Two-Piece Grey/Lavender Silk Ensemble in Presentation Box
Of grey and lavender striped silk with narrow black shadow band, the ensemble comprises very elaborately constructed jacket with built-in blouse; the blouse with box-pleated silk front and muslin sides and back, the jacket with full muslin lining, flared front with unusual double row of collar ruffles on one side offset by same double row of ruffles forming a faux-pocket on the other side. The dart-shaped jacket back has interior ties for snug fit, and reverse box-pleated tail decorated with lavish lavender silk taffeta bow. With self-piped collar with lace trim, lace edging at sides, 1/2 length fitted sleeves with lace edging. And full skirt with muslin waistband, hook and eye closure, lace edging at hemline. In boutique presentation box with fashion engraving on lid. 4" shoulder width. 6" waist. 8" skirt length. Circa 1870.

149. Tiny Mull Gown with Rose Cotton Sateen Under-Dress
The two-piece gown is constructed of rose cotton sateen under ruche of delicate white mull, having a fitted bodice with low-rounded neckline, short puffed sleeves, elaborately attached "froth" of mull decorated with lavender silk edging, ribbons and fine white lace, hook and eye closure; with matching skirt having stiffened muslin attached-petticoat, rose cotton sateen underskirt, mull overskirt with lavender silk banding and bows, hook and eye closure. 2 1/4" shoulder width. 3 1/2" waist. 6" skirt length. Circa 1865.

150. Ivory Silk Capote Bonnet with Bavolet
Of ivory silk taffeta with wire-framed front, the bonnet has elaborately gathered and pleated crown and sides, box-pleated bavolet, self-ruching at top with scalloped edging, gathered lace and silk ribbon trim, net and silk lining, ivory silk ties. 2 1/2" facial width. Circa 1870.

151. Lavender Striped Grenadine Two-Piece Gown
Of very fine grenadine in a narrow lavender/grey pinstripe, the two-piece ensemble comprises dart-shaped camargo basque whose sides are drawn up into horizontal pleats and whose reverse-box-pleated back has elaborate bustle achieved by constructed gathers, 3/4 length sleeves with turn-up cuffs, lavender silk collar and revers, purple velvet bow at back, upper muslin

lining. With full skirt having flat front, gathered back, self-piping at hem, muslin waist, hook and eye closure. 4 1/2" shoulder width. 7" waist. 9" skirt front. 12" skirt back. Circa 1870.

152. Tarlatan Bonnet with Lavender Ribbons in Original Box
Double-wire-framed bonnet of stiffened tarlatan with padded gathered interior is so richly covered with lace-edged cotton batiste gathered borders as to nearly cover the muslin, with double row batiste bavolet, and lavender silk ribbons, streamers and ribbon loops. In original hat box labelled "Au Quatre Coins/Mennier...". Circa 1870.

153. Ivory-handled Purple Silk Parasol
With carved ivory handle and tip, the eight-pronged parasol which opens and closes has original silk/taupe striped cover with silk fringe trim. 8" L. Circa 1865.

154. Ivory Silk and Mull Two-Piece Gown
Of ivory silk satin with overlay of stripe-woven silk voile, the gown comprises dart-fitted front and back bodice with diagonal bands of voile, 1/2 length double-seamed sleeves with turn-up lace cuffs, lace collar, full muslin lining, hook and loop closure. With ivory silk satin gathered tie-back skirt overlaid in elaborately caught-up gathers of silk voile, pleated mull balayeuse, full muslin lining with interior ties for "shaping" the gathers. The bodice is attached to skirt with long silk ribbons which helps "arrange" the mull skirt gathers. 5" shoulder width. 8" waist. 10" skirt front. Circa 1865.

155. Mauve Silk Taffeta Gown
The one-piece gown of mauve silk taffeta has low-rounded neckline with self-piping and lace stand-up collar interwoven with narrow black velvet ribbons, gathered bodice, short set-in sleeves with double row of self-ruffles edged with black velvet and lace trim, set-in waistband. Elaborately constructed skirt whose flat-front panel is decorated with wide diagonal bands of black velvet and taffeta and velvet bows, and whose two flat-cut side panels and gathered back panel are decorated with ruffled bands of taffeta edged with black velvet. Cotton sateen-lined bodice, stiffened muslin-lined skirt, hook and loop closure, pleated balayeuse. With 5" wide constructed taffeta bow for attaching at back waist. 6 1/2" shoulder width. 8" waist. 16" overall. Circa 1870.

156. Linen Two-Piece Summer Ensemble
Of natural color linen, the two-piece ensemble comprises cuirass basque whose box pleats at front and back allow the jacket to slightly flare over the hips, with wide collar below self-corded neckline, button front, long double-seamed sleeves with turn-up cuffs. With matching skirt having muslin waistband, flat front, cartridge pleating at sides and back, hook and eye closure, an applied band of box pleats which extend around the hemline, another band of self-ruffles above the hemline, and short bands of those same pleats and ruffles at the center of skirt front panel just below the jacket length; overall decoration of handmade rick-rack, embroidery and lace. 4" shoulders. 7" waist. 11" skirt. Circa 1870.

157. Blue Cotton Percale Day Dress
Of navy blue cotton Percale printed with ecru dots, the one-piece dress has fully-muslin-lined bodice and long double-seamed sleeves, self-banded neckline trimmed with handmade rick-rack, eight buttons and hand-made buttonholes, cream embroidery on dress front and faux cuffs. The back has dart-shaping above the waist and reverse double-box-pleated sweep-length skirt. 5" shoulder width. 8" waist. 15" front length. Circa 1870.

158. Blue Satin Duchesse Ensemble and Undergarments
Of cornflower-blue silk satin duchesse, the ensemble comprises form-fitted bodice with dart-shaping, slightly-flared peplum, six lacing holes at front bodice with ivory grosgrain silk ribbons criss-crossing over the box-pleated plastron, muslin and lace modesty panel, silk ribbon lacing, double-seam long sleeves with lace faux-cuffs, brown sateen lining, hook and eye closure. With matching skirt having four alternate panels: flat-cut, undecorated box-pleated, decorated box-pleated with criss-crossed silk ribbons, and ruffled tiered lace interwoven with silk ribbons, balayeuse, cotton sateen lining. The skirt back is slightly gathered with deeply-flounced overskirt. With three matching cotton muslin undergarments (chemise, petticoat, pantalets). 6" shoulder width. 8 1/2" waist. 14" skirt length. Circa 1880.

159. White Jaconet Cotton Day Dress
The delicate white block-patterned cotton, printed with small blue dots, forms a princess-line gown whose jacket front is stitched closed below the hips; with lace-edged eased neckline, double-seam set-in sleeves, dart-shaped back bodice, tiny gathers at back waist, sweep-length skirt. Decorations include bands of pleats at cuffs and shoulder seams which extend onto back bodice, and wider band of stitched-down pleats at hemline. 4 1/2" shoulder seam. 13" front length. Circa 1870.

161. Blue Silk Wire-Framed Coronet Bonnet
Of blue silk taffeta with black pencil stripe, the narrow coronet-shaped bonnet has wire-shaping designed to give height to very tip of bonnet, narrow black velvet banding and ties, black velvet bows, black lace trim, muslin lining. To fit 2" facial width. Circa 1865.

160. Three-Piece Blue Taffeta Gown with Capeline Bonnet
Of crisp blue silk taffeta and blue velvet, the ensemble comprises short dart-fitted basque slightly flared below the waist, set-in double-seam sleeves with velvet faux cuffs, eight silk-covered decorative buttons, hook and eye closure, subdued lace trim. With demi-train skirt having flat front, box-pleating and gathers at sides and back (the bottom half of skirt lined with stiffened fabric for shape), and added wide ruffle of blue silk bordered by blue velvet ribbon at lower skirt. With fine-muslin-lined blue velvet polonaise, edged with blue silk, longer in front, pulled up by horizontal pleats at the back and decorated with large blue and velvet bow. With capeline bonnet designed to perch at the back of the head by its egg-shaped firm silk-twill covered frame, with gathered twill interior, extended length blue velvet back which covers the neck, handmade lace trim, fabric flowers, silk streamers. 4 1/2" shoulder width. 8" waist. 9 1/2" front skirt length. Circa 1868.

162. Fine White Muslin Three-Piece Gown
The three-piece ensemble features dart-shaped hip-length fully-lined basque with fraise at the V-shaped neckline, placket front with hidden hook and eye closure, long narrow sleeves with lace cuffs. With cartridge-pleated skirt having set-in waistband and extra ruffle at hemline. And polonaise with constructed box-pleated flounce at back, ruching and narrow bands of ruffles and lace at front. 4 1/2" shoulder width. 7" waist. 10" skirt length. Circa 1870.

163. White Fur Muff and Royal Palatine in Original Presentation Box
White fur palatine with brown tails has silk padded lining; with matching muff having ivory and mauve braided cord. In original glass-front presentation box with lace edging. Circa 1875.

164. Aqua Silk Capote Bonnet, Fur Muff and Bone Folding Fan
Wire-framed capote bonnet is lavishly covered with aqua silk arranged in gathers, drapes and folds, decorated with gold beetle button, aqua silk streamers, cord neck catch, ivory silk lining. 2" face width. And white long fur muff with padded ivory interior, aqua silk twill ties. 2" W. And 11-blade bone folding fan with decorative floral painted designs. Circa 1875.

165. White Mull Two-Piece Ensemble with Demi-Train
Of sheer white mull, comprising cuirass basque with fitted bodice, set-in waistband, dart-shaped back, rounded low neckline with lace fraise, long narrow sleeves with trumpet-shaped open cuffs designed to partially cover the hands, flared peplum, extended-length back of jacket with constructed bustle below an attached gathered and lace trimmed over-flap; the jacket trimmed with band of lace-edged ruching. With matching skirt with set-in waistband, demi-train with lace-edged hemline, wide band of lace-edged ruching at lower skirt. 4" shoulder. 7" waist. 10" front skirt length. Circa 1872.

166. Rose Kid Gloves and Folding Fan
Soft kid gloves in delicate rose color have stitched fingers, set-in thumb, scalloped edging, 2 1/2" L. And carved bone folding fan with 8 hand-painted blades interwoven with rose silk ribbon, brass wrist loop, 2" L. Circa 1880.

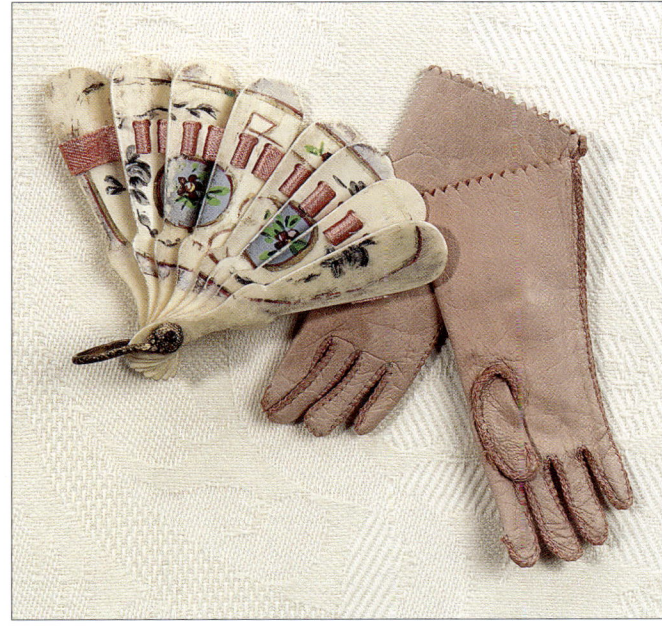

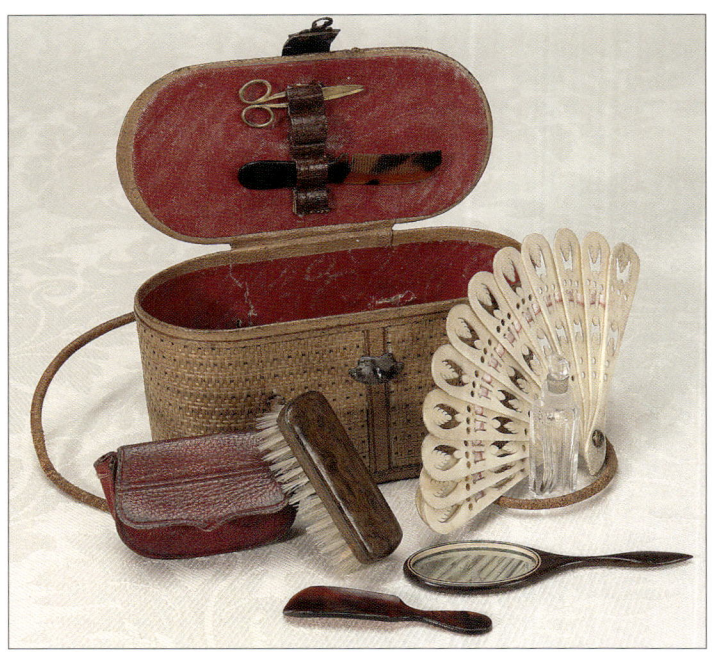

167. White Cotton Matelasse Pardessus
Of lozenge-patterned white cotton matelasse, the hip-length fitted pardessus has dart-shaped back with flaring at the hips, full-length box-pleats down the front which are stitched down for shaping at the waist, placket front with buttons/button holes and cutwork and embroidered trim, double-seamed curved long sleeves, rolled collar and cuffs. 5" shoulder width. 8" waist. Circa 1868.

168. Woven Toilette Case
The tiny-patterned woven cane valise has leather banding and trim, silver clasp and rosette, leather handles, hinges open to reveal red silk-paper interior with various toiletry items including miniature brush, comb, mirror, scissors, purse, fan, perfume bottle. 4 1/2" L. Circa 1865.

169. White Cotton Pique Fashion Dress for Child
The lower-calf-length princess-style dress is composed of eleven alternating bands of white pique and Battenberg lace, each seam edged with narrow braid. With white box "kick" pleats at back hemline, rounded collar with four rows of lace or braid, long narrow sleeves with braid trim, wide row of Battenberg lace at hemline, hidden button closure at front placket. 3 3/4" shoulder width. 13" overall length. Circa 1875.

Chapter IV

Child or Bebe Doll Dresses
1875 - 1895

66

170. Aqua Challis Wool Dress
The princess-styled dress has flared jacket front with inset-center panel, mancheron sleeves that criss-cross at the top, panel of wide-pleats at the lower back. The jacket edges, sleeves and front and back panels are trimmed with narrow ivory silk braid and 1/2" fine lace; and wide silk grosgrain bows decorate the front panel and shoulders. Muslin lining, hook and eye closure. 3 1/2" shoulder width. 8" princess-style waist. 10" overall. Circa 1878.

171. Pale Green Challis Wool Dress
The princess-styled dress has flared jacket front with full-length inset center front panel; panel of box pleats at the lower back; long double-seamed, curved sleeves with faux cuffs. With elaborate broderie Anglaise decorations, cotton lining, hook and eye closure. 4 1/2" shoulder width. 9" princess-style waist. 11" overall length. Circa 1878.

172. Ivory Twill Silk Coat Dress
The princess-styled coat dress has jacket-front with flared sides, four-panel form-fitting back with defined waist, panel of narrow box pleats below the back hips, long double-seam curved coat sleeves, square-cut collar with box-pleated tulle fraise. The dress is trimmed with bands of openwork handmade lace over peach silk bands, lace edging at collar and cuffs, peach silk bows. Cotton sateen lining, hook and eye closure. 4" shoulder width. 10" princess-style waist. 10" overall length. Circa 1878.

173. Pale Green Challis Wool Dress
The modified princess-style dress has dart-shaped front panel and V-shaped neckline edged with openwork lace which continues down the jacket-front; 1" band at hips borders two rows of narrow box pleats; double-seam long sleeves; shapely back with curved side panels which center a 3/4 length center-back panel of partially sewn-down pressed pleats that contrast narrow kick pleats at the hemline. The dress is trimmed with ivory cord piping at shoulders, front hip belt and back seam lines, and with lace trim at collar, cuffs, and all edges. Muslin lining, hook and eye closure. 3 1/2" shoulder width. 9" princess-style waist. 9" overall length. Circa 1880.

174. Aqua Albatross Wool Dress with Hip Sash
The princess-style dress has double-panel flared front, rounded neckline, faux collar of silk faille stripes edged by 3/4" band of cotton lace, stitched-down hip sash with V-shaped edging, double row of narrow aqua box pleats, silk grosgrain-covered buttons, cotton lace balayeuse and faux cuffs, dart-shaped button back, muslin lining. 4 1/2" shoulder width. 10" princess waist. 10" overall length. Circa 1882.

175. White Pique Princess-Style Dress
Of very narrow horizontally-ribbed white pique the one-piece dress has princess-style shaping with snugly-fitted top and flared skirt, faux-double-breasted construction with double row of pearl buttons but only one row of button holes, square-cut neckline, 3/4 length double-seamed coat sleeves, the pleated skirt-back opens for dressing and hooks closed, with back V-shaped decorative flaps, two faux-pockets on front. The dress is edged at collar, cuffs, button front, pockets, and back flaps with scalloped-edge cotton with embroidered pinwheel cut-outs, with edging of cotton braid. 4" shoulder width. 12" princess waist. 11" length. Circa 1880.

176. White Patterned Woven Cotton Princess-Style Dress
Of white silky cotton with alternating open and closed woven bands, the jacket dress has princess styling, two flared front panels and four narrow back panels with definition of the waist, double-seam 3/4 length sleeves with cut-work cotton cuffs. There are two cut-work pockets with lace edging set very low on dress so as to appear as a decorative band, and a matching actual band at back of dress, double row of cotton dust ruffles at hemline, cutwork rolled collar and placket edging, lace trim, pearl buttons/button holes. 3" shoulder width. 9" princess waist. 9" overall length. Circa 1882.

177. White Cotton Pique Princess-Style Dress
Of horizontally ribbed very narrow white pique, the princess-style coat dress has full length faux-placket front with broderie Anglaise center bordered by bands of embroidered cotton ruffles; lace fraise at rounded neckline above the 2" collar; 3/4 length double-seamed sleeves trimmed with three borders of cutwork and embroidery at cuffs; band of inverted box pleats at hemline with embroidered border; dart-shaped back with ten buttons/button holes. 4" shoulder width. 11" princess waist. 12" overall length. Circa 1880.

178. Blue Cotton Chambray Princess-Style Dress
Of sturdy but fine-woven pale blue cotton chambray, the jacket-style dress has front panel constructed of four bands of knife tucks separated by self-fabric bands and edged by ruffled Valenciennes lace, and closed by row of six buttons/button holes, pompadour-style bodice with lace edging, elbow-length sleeves with double row of ruffled lace, two rows of knife pleats around front and sides of skirt bottom with lace edging on each. Fourteen rows of narrow knife tucks extend the length of back and are basted down at the waistline, large lace-edged self bow at derriere. 4 1/2" shoulder width. 13 1/2" princess waist. 10 1/2" overall length. Circa 1880.

179. White Muslin Pinafore
Of fine white muslin with open-back, the pinafore has rounded neck, epaulet sleeves with open tops, bodice pleats held down by stitched front waistband, pleated front skirt, two pockets, five rows of tucking around the hemline, gathers at back collar with loosely falling back. Long apron ties, scalloped-edge embroidered cotton at waist, pocket tops and neckline, double-row of same at sleeves. 3 1/2" shoulder width. 9" overall length. Circa 1880.

180. Ivory and Mauve Silk Velvet Coat and Bonnet
Of lustrous silk-velvet with unusual ivory and mauve checkered pattern, the princess-style coat has faux double-breasted front; four glass buttons with button holes off-setting another row of same buttons, small rounded collar, double-seamed sleeves, walking slit at bottom back trimmed by three matching glass buttons, polished cotton lining. 4" shoulder width. 9" waist. 12" overall length. With paquebot capote bonnet of ivory twill silk having curved crown and back, flat sides, double row of gathered Valenciennes lace around the face with fabric rose petals, lace streamers, silk lining. Circa 1875.

181. Lavender Linsey-Woolsey Dress and Cap with Boots
The faux-double-breasted coat-dress has princess styling, seven buttons with handmade button holes, rounded collar with pointed front tips and handmade lace edging; double-seamed sleeves with roll-up cuffs and handmade lace edging; two large rounded pockets with handmade lace edging; dart-shaped upper back with set-in waist hidden by wide peach silk grosgrain sash and bow, three wide inverted-box-pleats

below the back waist; cotton sateen lining. With matching Tam O'Shanter cap with wide pleats captured into a banded edge, rosette trim, net lining. 4 1/2" shoulder width. 9" princess waist. 12" overall length. With soft white kid leather boots, having three pairs of grommets, cored lace, silk rosette, brown kid soles marked "6". 2 1/2" L. Circa 1875.

183. Two Bonnets and Black Leather Boots
Straw Bonnet with wide brim, flat top is trimmed with a confection of rose batiste cotton edged with Valenciennes lace, trimmed with maroon silk bow, ivory pleated silk on inside brim and as lining, with neck cord, 2" inside diam. Wire-framed maroon velvet bonnet with wide brim having rolled edge, flat top, velvet band and ribbons, white feather, stitched-down gathers of rose silk twill inside the brim and as lining, 2" inside diam. Black leather boots edged in brown thread, four lacing holes, rose silk laces, leather soles marked "6" with rose openwork laced stockings, 2 1/2" L. Circa 1875.

184. Pale Green Silk Dress and Lace Cap
Very delicate pale green silk-twill princess-style dress has button front with nine buttons/button holes, self-banded round neckline with lace fraise, double-seamed long sleeves designed to cover the tops of hands, V-shaped opening at the wrist, faux cuffs, handmade lace trim; dart-shaped waist with defined waist. The entire hemline of dress is trimmed with van-dyking above four rows of slightly-ruffled lace, above a band of narrow silk twill pleats. 5" shoulder width. 13" princess waist. 15" overall length. With fine tulle-over-silk cap constructed in narrow bands of tulle, gathered detail of silk lending a padded effect, three rows of ruffled lace at crown alternating with narrow loops of ribbon, three silk decorative bows, hidden adjustable ties inside the cap. Circa 1875.

185. Lace and Silk Ribbon Bonnet
The bonnet is constructed of alternating bands of embroidered fine muslin, guipure lace, and muslin with interwoven ivory silk ribbons; the constructed back-of-head circle has embroidered rose-on-tulle with interwoven silk ribbon border and ruffle of lace; three pleated lace ruffles and ivory silk ribbons frame the face with added ruffle at crown, silk satin bows and streamers, muslin lining around the inside edges, hidden adjustable ties. About 5 1/2" facial width. Circa 1875.

186. Lace and Tulle Bonnet
The bonnet is constructed of narrow bands of tulle overlaid by slightly ruffled bands of scalloped-edge tulle and bordered by narrow interwoven ivory silk ribbons; the constructed back-of-head circle is of tulle with embroidered flower and ruffled lace border; triple-box-pleated lace ruffles at the crown are decorated with silk ivory ribbon loops; ivory silk ribbon streamers. About 4" facial width. Circa 1875.

187. Pale Blue Challis Wool Dress and Lace Cap
Of pale blue fine challis wool, the princess-style dress has seven buttons/hand-made button holes down the center front, rounded neckline with self-piping and hand-crocheted collar; mancheron sleeves that criss-cross at top trimmed with self-piping, with fine-muslin elbow-length engageantes trimmed with featherstitch and hand-crochet; two front pockets bordered in ivory silk; border of very narrow pleats at hemline set-off by clustered ivory silk ribbon; dart-shaped back with ivory silk sash and bow. Full muslin lining. 5" shoulder width. 10" princess waist. 12" overall length. Circa 1878. With elaborate lace cap constructed of bands of lace alternating with crochetwork interwoven with ribbons, lace circle at back of head, tightly ruffled lace border, extra lace ruffle and silk ribbons at crown, muslin border lining and streamers. 4" face width.

188. Pair, Matching Fine-Muslin Pinafores
Of fine muslin, the matching princess-style pinafores have low-rounded necklines trimmed with scalloped edging and ruffled cutwork, cutwork scalloped capelet sleeves, 15 full-length vertical tucks, three horizontal tucks along the hemline, button and loop at back neckline, open back. 4 1/2" shoulder width. 9" overall length. Circa 1880.

189. White Cotton Pique Princess-Style Dress
Of very narrow ribbed white cotton pique, the princess-style coat dress has three full-length rows of tucks on either side of placket front with eight buttons/button holes and trimmed with scalloped cutwork cotton, matching rounded collar, 3/4 length double-seamed sleeves with rolled cuffs, unusual shaping-seam 1/4 way down the sleeve, shaping-darts at back terminating in constructed jacket tails and inverted box pleats, cutwork trim around hemline. 5" shoulder width. 11" princess waist. 13" overall length. Circa 1880.

190. Tulle Lace Bonnet with Cotton Lining
The bonnet is constructed of alternating bands of tulle lace and circular-woven lace, with set-in circular back with tiny embroidered circles, wide band of pleated lace ruffles around the brim, cluster of lace gathers and silk ribbon loops at crest, ivory silk grosgrain bows and streamers, fine cotton lining with cotton lace edging, adjustable hidden ties. 5" facial width. Circa 1880.

191. Tulle Lace Bonnet with Pique Lining
Constructed of narrow bands of circular woven lace overlaid periodically with ruffled lace and interwoven silk ribbons, ruffled cotton border around the face below generously-gathered lace ruffles, extra cluster of lace ruffles at crown with looped silk ribbons, pique cap lining with adjustable ties, muslin streamers. 5" facial width. Circa 1880.

191A. Ivory Silk Capote Bonnet with Original French Label
Ivory silk wire-brimmed bonnet with double ruffled brim that encloses the side of face has pleated soft back, ivory silk bows, braid trim, ivory silk streamers, silk lining with original gold lettering "Specialities de les Enfants, A L'Eclair, ...Paris". To fit 3" facial width. Circa 1880.

192. White Dotted Swiss Princess Dress
Of sheer white dotted Swiss, the princess-style dress has pompadour neckline, front center panel with full-length hook and eye closures hidden by the double row of lace-edged ruffles that cover the panel seams and extend around the entire neckline; there are four additional bands of horizontal double-ruffles with lace edging at the front. With 3/4 length unusual triple-seam sleeves, triple-ruffled cuffs with lace edging, double thickness of fabric at top 2/3 of back with two rows of double ruffles. The hemline is trimmed with lace-edged double ruffles centering a band of ruching. 9 1/2" shoulder width. 18" princess-style waist. 22" overall length. Circa 1882.

193. Wide-Brimmed Straw Watteau Bonnet with Velvet Ribbons
The woven straw bonnet has flattened top with sunken center, graduated-width wire-framed brim which is very narrow at the back to accommodate the coiffure, and very wide at the sides and face for modesty; the side brims are flattened against the head and the front brim tilts upward in duck-tail fashion. Three bands of cherry-red velvet ribbons band the crown, criss-crossing at the top and cascading into long streamers, cherry fruit and leaves decorate one side and a large velvet bow the other. The interior is muslin-lined. 4" head width. Circa 1875.

194. Three-Color Woven Straw Duck-Bill Bonnet
Of woven narrow bands of three-color straw, the bonnet has snug-fitted cap, brim-less back, and extended-length front brim; a profusion of picot-edged narrow red silk grosgrain ribbons and bows trim the crown, double streamer-ties. 2" head width. Circa 1880.

195. White Cotton Faille Dress with Broderie Anglaise Panels
The princess-styled jacket dress is constructed of sewn-together alternating bands of narrow-ribbed cotton and broderie Anglaise featuring cutwork, embroidery and fagoting, and a front panel of broderie Anglaise joined by white braid and arranged on the bias, low-rounded collar of braid and narrow scallop-edged broderie Anglaise, box-pleated cotton twill lower skirt. Border of scalloped-edge broderie Anglaise are along the jacket and skirt edges, and form a Bertha collar and short sleeves; seven buttons/button holes on one front side, seven decorative buttons on the other. 8 1/2" shoulder width. 23" princess waist. 20" overall length. Circa 1880.

196. White Cotton Faille Dress with Low Pockets
The princess-styled dress has button closure bordered by full-length broderie Anglaise panels edged in white braid; the same broderie Anglaise forms a dentelled Bertha collar, short sleeves, and skirt ruffle; an added skirt ruffle at derriere emphasizes an ivory silk decoration. The low-rounded neckline is edged with cord and narrow broderie Anglaise. Two pockets at the lower hips are edged with cord and decorated with band of dentelled broderie Anglaise. 8 1/2" shoulder width. 24" princess waist. 20 1/2" overall length. Circa 1880.

197. Black Leather Shoes, Size 12, with Heels
Black leather slipper-style shoe with low-cut vamp has stiffened muslin lining, black fabric edging, very soft brown kid soles with darker brown outer rims (in the manner of Huret-made shoes), applied shaped wooden low heels, impressed "12". 4" L. Circa 1878.

198. White Grenadine Cotton Frock and Felt Hat
Of white cotton grenadine with pulled-thread vertical striping, the summer dress has square-cut bodice with self-banding, mancheron sleeves which overlap at top, covered by moire silk shoulder knots, picot-edged alencon silk edges neckline and sleeves, slightly-gathered bodice, slightly-high waist with set-in waistband, box-pleated skirt with flat front and kilt pleats at back, moire silk skirt bow, hook and eye closure. 4 1/2" shoulder width. 9 1/2" waist. 10 1/2" length. With felt hat having rounded crown, turned-up stiffened brim whose underside is covered with pleated bronze silk, ivory flow-flow ribbons, alencon lace ruffle; ivory silk lining, grosgrain banding and bow, cord throat tie. Circa 1880.

199. Black Leather Shoes for Early Bru Bebe
Of soft black leather, the square-toed shoes have ankle straps with black button and loop closures, brown silk banding and bow, silver buckle trim, muslin lining, light tan leather soles. Signed "B" in script in oval, and "2". 2 1/2" L. Circa 1878.

200. Black Leather Shoes signed Bru Jne, Size 4
Of soft black leather, the round-toed shoes have ankle straps with black button closure, brown silk banding, black leather "bow" with silver buckle in the center, twill lining, brown soles. Signed "Bru Jne Paris" and "4". 2 1/4" L. Circa 1882.

201. Black Leather Shoes signed Bru Jne, Size 1
Of soft black leather, identically styled to #200. Signed "Bru Jne Paris" and "1". 1 3/4" L. Circa 1882.

202. Ivory Silk Satin Capeline Bonnet
Of lustrous ivory silk satin duchesse, the bonnet has wire-brim overlaid by double-row of wire brim with richly-gathered satin decorated with pleated picot-edged tulle and satin ribbon flow-flow, soft crown decorated with soutache in floral patterns, large silk bow, box-pleated bavolet edged with narrow crimped ribbons, long silk ribbon ties, lining, grosgrain interior banding. To fit face width 5". Circa 1880.

203. Maroon and Flowered Ivory Silk Jacket Dress
Of maroon silk satin, the intricately constructed dress has plastron with five pleats and narrow band of ruching at the bottom, dress sides with narrower pleating clustered at the sides of waistline and six rows of smocking that extend around the sides to meet the set-in flowered ivory silk panels at the back of dress; maroon silk panniers and polonaise over floral-patterned silk pleated underskirt; another border of box-pleated maroon silk is at the hemline as well as muslin and lace pleated balayeuse. Floral-patterned ivory silk full-length lapels with self-cording evolve into a wide collar, the back center panels extend into

two tails, double-seam coat sleeves have ivory silk cuffs of graduated width; ivory silk box pleats and lace fraise trim the neckline. Muslin lining, hook and eye closure. 5 1/2" shoulder width. 12" waist. 13" overall length. Circa 1884.

203A. Fingerless Lace Gloves in Original Box
Arranged with their original store box with gilt-edging are a pair of handmade lace fingerless gloves with defined thumb, scalloped edging, open-work at wrist. 2 3/4" L. glove. Circa 1885.

204. White Marseilles Cotton Dress
With flannel-back and tiny waffle-weave pattern, the princess-style dress has muslin-banded low-rounded neckline edged with broderie Anglaise, wide cutwork ruffled and scalloped-edge Bertha collar, four-panel dress with six full-length box pleats, and band of short box pleats at the hemline; mancheron sleeves wider at bottom than top, with cotton banding and broderie Anglaise edging, six-button closure hidden under back box pleat. 6 1/2" shoulder width. 16 1/2" princess waist. 16 1/2" overall length. Circa 1880.

205. White Chambray Calash Bonnet
The collapsible frame bonnet is constructed of six oval-looped wires allowing the bonnet to fold flat or expand, covered with ruched white chambray, with wide beret-style back centered by hand-tatted panel, graduated-width goffering ruffle around the face overlaid by ruffled self-border with tatted edge, streamers. To fit 6" face width. Circa 1880.

206. Brown Silk Quilted Bonnet
Of very rich chocolate brown silk, padded and lined for soft thickness, the bonnet is quilted in lozenge pattern, band of pleated Valenciennes lace around the edge held by narrow brown silk ribbon, similar lace border around the back of head with large brown bow, pleated muslin crown with lace edging and brown silk bow. To fit 4 1/2" face width. Circa 1880.

207. Lace Ruffled Cap
Constructed in a very intricate manner of alternate bands of embroidered tulle and beading lace with ivory silk ribbons, circle of tatted lace at back of head, double row of pleated lace encircling the cap front and neck, an extra ruffle, flow-flow and ivory silk grosgrain bows at crown, ivory silk streamers, the cap is designed to enclose the back of head and to frame the face with lace. To fit 4 1/2" face width. Circa 1885.

208. Straw Hat with Faux-Straw Border
Circular hat with low rounded crown is formed from narrow alternating bands of woven straw and stiffened buckram; with wide brim constructed of five bands of alternating woven straw, stiffened buckram and an outside border of stiffened passementerie. Ivory silk ribbons decorates the outer brim. Muslin lining, cord ties. Fits 7" head circumference. Circa 1880.

209. Straw Rubens Hat with Maroon and Red Silk Trim
Constructed of narrow bands of woven straw, with rounded flat-topped crown and upturned brim, the outside is decorated with red grosgrain band and streamer, red silk rosette; the inside is decorated with maroon-silk-lined brim and red rosette, net lining. Fits 6 1/2" head circumference. Circa 1885.

210. Flat Straw Hat with Wide Front Brim
Constructed of narrow bands of woven straw with outer border of criss-crossed open-weave straw, rounded flat-top crown; the outside decorated with black velvet bows and floral monture; the inside-brim lined with black velvet; buckram lining. Fits 9 1/2" head circumference. Circa 1885.

211. Black Leather Shoes signed L.P.
Soft black leather shoes with ankle straps that fasten with silver buttons and loops, black leather bows with silver buckles, leather soles, signed L.P., size 6. 2 1/4" L. Circa 1880.

212. Black Leather Shoes signed C.M.
Soft black leather shoes with ankle straps, double black bead and loops closure, brown banding, brown silk rosettes, signed C.M., size 1. Circa 1880. 2" L.

213. Tan Leather Shoes with Boutique Label
Light tan soft leather shoes with ankle straps and double silver button closure, silk rosettes, royal blue insteps, tan soles, signed 1. With partial original paper label "A La Poupee...". Circa 1880. 2 1/2" L.

214. Tan Leather Boots and Lisle Stockings
Of soft tan leather with overcast edging, three pairs of lacing grommets, original cord lace, brown leather bow and silver buckle, signed "8". With open-weave lisle stockings having woven-in heel, toe and top. 2 1/2" L. Circa 1885.

215. Straw Beehive Bonnet with Wide Brim
Constructed of very narrow bands of woven straw, with rounded crown sunken at center, very wide brims with turned-up front brim; the outside decorated with wide maroon moire taffeta ribbons and narrow black velvet ribbons that extend to tie under the chin. Fits 7 1/2" head circumference. Circa 1885.

216. White Fur Muff in Presentation Box
White fur muff with lush padding, lining, has decorative tails, is contained in original presentation green paper cylinder box to exactly fit the muff, with lid and carrying string, engraving of child holding flowers. 5" W. Circa 1880.

217. Red Wool Hood with Wool Slipper Stockings
Red wool hand-knitted hood has decorative knots, scalloped open-work edging, strings en coulisse at neckline with tassel tips, scalloped bavolet. With thick woven slippers in form of boots (2 1/2" L.) having cord rosettes and drawstring tops. To fit 3" W. head.

218. White Cotton Ten-Piece Wardrobe
Comprising Swiss muslin dress with dropped waist and lantern sleeves, trimmed with box-shaped cutwork and broderie Anglaise, with matching Swiss muslin pinafore whose straps are formed of embroidered lattice lace; cotton faille princess-style dropped waist frock with soutache embroidered center panel trimmed with lace, box-pleated skirt, double-seam curved coat sleeves with soutache trimmed fold-up cuffs, small rolled collar with soutache trim, button back; plus another pinafore with bretelle sleeves; muslin night shift; knickers with gathered cuffs; full slip with blue silk ribbon trim and Valenciennes lace; three similar petticoats with strings en coulisse, cutwork trim. 4 1/2" shoulder width. 10 1/2" waist. 9" overall length muslin dress. Circa 1885.

219. French Tan Leather Boots by Alart, size 5
Tan leather boots with overcast edges, three pairs of metal-edged grommets, original cord lace with metal tip, pom-pom decoration, signed with figure of doll in chemise, for Alart, Paris. Size 5. 2" L. Circa 1885.

220. French White Leather Boots by Alart, size 6
White leather boots with curved tops, overcast stitching along the edges, three pairs of metal-edged grommets, white laces with metal tips, white pom-poms, leather soles, signed with figure of doll in chemise, for Alart, Paris. Size 6. 2 1/2" L. Circa 1885.

221. French Dark Brown Leather Boots by Alart, size 10
Dark brown leather boots with overcast light brown edging, five pairs of lacing holes made without metal grommets, maroon cord laces with metal tips, brown pom-pom. Signed with figure of doll in chemise for Alart, Paris. Size 10. 3 1/2" L. Circa 1885.

222. French Tan Leather Boots by Alart, size 11
Tan leather boots with overcast curved tops and fronts have four pairs of metal-edged lacing grommets, original cord laces with metal tips, pom-pom, signed with figure of doll in chemise for Alart, Paris. Size 11. 4" L. Circa 1885.

223. White Cotton Grenadine
Chemise Dress with Handmade Embroidery
Of fine white cotton interwoven with tiny mesh bands, the princess-style dress has square-cut collar edged with braid and guipure lace, front and back hip-length box pleats which are periodically basted down to hold their shape, two rows of braid at hips above additional box pleats at front and back, rectangular-shaped faux-panniers at sides of hips, button/buttonholes and hook and eye closures down full length of back. The dress is trimmed with borders of handmade embroidery with dents de loup edging, and red and blue cross-stitch and feathered patterns. The embroidery borders form the Bertha collar, epaulette sleeves, hip belt and edges of panniers. 4" shoulder width. 10 1/2" princess waist. 12" overall length. Circa 1882.

224. Indigo Blue Polished Muslin Frock
Of very fine tightly-woven cotton with slight lustrous finish, the drop-waist dress has simple rounded neckline from which falls three wide pleats bordered by a curved self-ruffle; below the hips are two rows of narrow pleats which extend around the dress. Dart-shaped back-bodice with three buttons/buttonholes, double-seamed 3/4 length coat sleeves, pleated sash with two large decorative flaps at back. The sleeves, flaps, skirt pleats and bodice ruffle are edged with handmade lace with fagoting and picot detail. 3 1/4" shoulder width. 8 1/2" hips. 6 1/2" overall length. Circa 1880.

225. Navy Blue Silk/Cotton Twill Mariner Frock
Of silk/cotton blend with twill pattern, the mariner-influenced dress has princess-style drop-waist bodice with graduated-width lapel front forming a round collar in the back, inset front panel, double-seam curved coat sleeves, box pleats below the hips. The lapels, panel, cuffs and hemline are decorated with applied very narrow bands of silk twill, picot-edged Alencon lace trims the upper collar and cuffs. 5" shoulder width. 16" hips. 10" overall length. Circa 1880.

226. White Percale Frock with Transfer Designs for Embroidery
Of slightly glazed white cotton percale, the high-waisted frock has high square-cut neckline, front bretelles with notched lapels that extend down the flat front of skirt in tablier style, double-seam curved coat sleeve with notched cuffs, pleated sides of skirt, fitted back bodice, gathered back skirt, waist ties that commence at sides of front and extend into long streamers at back. The dress is trimmed with argentan lace at neckline, cuffs and bretelles, has fabric-covered buttons, and stamped blue transfer designed to be embroidered. 7 1/4" shoulder width. 18" high waist. 18 1/2" overall length. Circa 1865.

227. White Nainsook Embroidered Frock with Bertha Collar
Of white nainsook the high-waisted frock has fitted front bodice with applied Bertha collar that extends around to back bodice which is constructed of narrow tucks, rounded neckline, lantern sleeves with graduated-width turn-up cuffs, set-in waistband with tucks, flat-front skirt, pleats at skirt sides, gathers at skirt back. The neckline, cuffs and bretelles are edged in Valenciennes border lace. The dress front, bretelles and cuffs are richly decorated with raised-pattern braid and delicate embroidered cutwork. 9 1/2" shoulder width. 22" high waist. 20" overall length. Circa 1880.

228. White Cotton Faille Gown
The white cotton faille princess-style gown, designed to fit snugly over the bodice, has low-rounded neckline, double-seamed curved coat sleeves, inset front panel of graduated width, set-in back yoke above nine box pleats that are basted down, back ties. Bands of insertion and scalloped-edge broderie Anglaise trim the front panel, cuffs, collar and form a double-border at front hemline. 6 1/2" shoulder width. 22" overall length. Circa 1880.

229. White Cotton Dimity Gown
Of sheer white cotton dimity the princess-styled gown has rounded neckline with embroidered band, slightly-full long sleeves with constructed tuck below the elbow and double fold-up lace-trimmed cuffs, princess-styling with inset front panel having rows of graduated-width tucks broken by periodic lace bands, tucks and lace at hemline, fitted back bodice with three buttons/buttonholes, gathered skirt. There is a ruffled lace-edged dimity Bertha collar and front panel border. With matching rose muslin liner. 4 3/4" shoulder width. 19" overall length. Circa 1885.

230. White Swiss Muslin Gown
Of white Swiss muslin with interwoven raised dots, the gown has fitted front and back yokes constructed of bands of muslin and lace, 3/4 length full sleeves with two bands of insertion lace at top of sleeve, gather front and back bodice bordered by lace and muslin bretelles, set-in waistband with cut-work for insertion of ribbon sash, long skirt of graduated-width entredeux-trimmed skirt, ruffled lace-trimmed borders at hemline and cuffs. With rose silk satin sash and rosettes, rose cotton sateen liner with matching lace trim, button/loop closures. 5" shoulder width. 26" length. Circa 1885.

231. Complete Trousseau for Child Doll
Arranged in gold-woven straw basket which is covered with ruffled and pleated Swiss muslin are the following: Swiss muslin baby gown with lace Bertha collar, tucks at bodice, sleeves and hem, insertion lace and beading trim, embroidered tulle skirt border, blue cotton voile lining, and matching ruffled-edge cap; long muslin slip, cotton button-front baby pants with set-in waistband, Swiss muslin lace-edged cover, flannel pad, washcloth, knit sacque with blue edging and tassels, two pairs of knit booties, cotton and cutwork short dress and matching chemise. With four accessories: glass bottle with knit wrapper, bone-handled baby rattle, bed-warmer, and little rubber toy pig with blue silk ribbon tie. 4 1/2" shoulder width. 18 1/2" length of gown. 9" length of dress. 18" x 13" basket. Circa 1885.

232. Embroidered Cotton Twill Bib-Collar in Presentation Box
Of narrow-ribbed cotton twill, the white rounded bib-collar has deeply-embossed embroidery patterns of flowers and leaves, self-piping at neckline, picot-edged lace border, button closure. In glass-fronted presentation box with gold ormulu paper trim. 6" neck. Circa 1880.

Chapter V

Best Dresses
1880 - 1895

233. Black Cotton Sateen Umbrella with Dog's Head Handle and Black Tulle and Straw Hat
The eight-metal-pronged umbrella with wooden handle and tip has brass figural dog's head grasp with sculptural detail of dog collar having (indecipherable) inscription, belt loops, black tassels, original black cotton sateen cover, contained in rich presentation box. 15" L. The woven black straw hat has high flat crown with curled straw trim, black soft cotton lining, wired brim of embroidered and beaded black tulle with black silk bow and feather. To fit 12 1/2" head circumference. Circa 1890.

234. White Fur Long-haired Collar and Muff
The circular collar is lined with padded ivory silk, has two button and loop closure; with matching silk-lined muff having white neck cord. To fit 10" neck. Circa 1890.

235. Winter-white Albatross Wool Two-Piece Dress
Having fitted bodice with V-shaped tucks and Alencon lace modesty panel, band collar, lantern sleeves with ruffled borders of Alencon lace having dentes de loup edging, muslin lined, hook and eye closure, two pleats at back sewn down at neckline and waist. With matching three-panel gored sweep-length skirt having flat front, flared back, decorated with five very narrow bands of silk ribbons, full muslin lining, placket opening at back, hook and eye closure. 6 1/2" shoulder width. 14" waist. 11" front skirt length. Circa 1880.

236. Black Leather Shoes signed with Hot Air Balloon
Black leather shoes have ankle straps with button and loop closure, brown overcast edging, card inner soles, brown silk rosettes, tan leather soles with incised edging, signed with insignia of hot air balloon labelled "Paris", and Marque Depose, size 10. 3 1/4" L. Circa 1890.

237. Black Leather Shoes signed with Star and Rays
Black leather shoes have low-cut vamp, ankle straps with button and loop closure, trimmed with brown overcast edging, brown silk rosettes, card inner soles, tan leather soles with incised edging, signed with insignia of star surrounded by rays enclosing words "Paris Bebe", Paris Depose, size 9. 3" L. Circa 1890.

238. Brown Leather Shoes signed with Script Letters
Brown leather shoes have high-cut vamp, ankle straps with silk button closures, overcast stitching, silk rosette to match buttons, yellow card soles, signed with Germanic script letters and "6". 2 1/2" L. Circa 1890.

239. Black Leather Shoes signed Louvre Bebe
Black leather shoes have ankle straps with button and hole closure, contrasting-brown overcast stitching on all edges, brown silk rosettes, half-fleece lined, card inner soles, brown soles with incised edging, signed "Louvre-Bebe, Modele Depose" with insignia and "6". 2 1/4" L. Circa 1890.

240. Royal Blue Velvet Dress and Hat
Comprising high-waisted dress with fitted bodice, box pleated skirt with inverted-box-pleat center panel, round collar with self-piping and cotton lace edging, lantern sleeves whose puffiness is achieved by form-fitted lining and banding, buckram-lined bodice, hook and eye closure. With matching hat having flat shallow crown and graduated-width brim very wide at the top, decorated with ivory silk satin ribbons on inside and outside brims, silk lining. 5" shoulder width. 17" yoke circ. 15" overall length. Circa 1885.

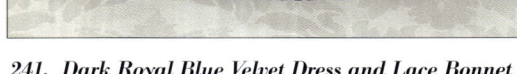

241. Dark Royal Blue Velvet Dress and Lace Bonnet
Of velvet, with stripe-cut pile, the drop-waist dress has box-pleated skirt, strings en coulisse low-rounded neckline, button back closure, silk twill-lined bodice, rose silk satin shoulder knots and hip bow. With lace bonnet constructed of alternating bands of Alencon and beading lace, the bands arranged in ray-like fashion from back-of-head lace circlet, the face framed by multiple borders of pleated tulle and lace, with extra borders at the crown decorated with flow-flow rose twill ribbons, border of rose twill banding and bows edges the sides and back of bonnet, rose twill streamers, silk lining. 8" shoulder width. 28" hip width. 19" overall length. Circa 1885.

242. Ivory Cotton Sateen Frock
Of silk-like cotton sateen, with fitted bodice, wide bretelle collar that centers plastron of very narrow knife pleats, round neckline, modified lantern sleeves with sewn-down narrow pleats at the elbow-length fitted cuffs, set-in waistband, gathered skirt with flat front panel; the bretelle, cuffs, waist, collar and hemline are decorated with cutwork muslin beading interwoven with rose silk picot-edged ribbons (a double row at waist), lace fraise at back neckline, fully-lined bodice, hook and eye closure. 3 1/2" shoulder width. 10" waist. 10 1/4" overall length. Circa 1885.

243. Rose Silk Capote Bonnet
Stiffened buckram form is covered with gathered rose silk which centers around a closely ruched back circlet, wire-framed brim with silk loops, silk lining, matelasse silk bows and streamers. To fit 5" face width. Circa 1890.

244. White Fur Muff-Purse with Tails
Of plush white fur with black tails, the muff-purse has small silver clasp at center top which opens to small kid-lined interior, with padded silk-lined muff, cord handle. 7" W. Circa 1890.

245. Straw Hat with Black Velvet Ribbons and Signed Bottines
The straw hat is woven in unusual rope and thread manner, having flat shallow crow, wide flat brim, band of black velvet with large bow and silver ornament; the underside decorated with elaborately ruched mousseline de soie, muslin lining. To fit 7 1/4" head circumference. With black leather bottines having two simple pairs of lacing holes with black lace, brown overcast stitching, leather soles impressed "Prime/L.Benoit/Bd. St.Michel 57 Paris", size 7", 2 3/4" L. Circa 1890.

246. White Angora Pelerine
Of long loopy-curled angora, the pelerine has ivory satin lining, decorated with two rose satin bows. 19" total length. Circa 1890.

247. Black Leather Shoes with Silver Buckles
Soft black leather with rounded shape, ankle straps with silver buttons and loops, black ribbon trim with beaded silver buckle, mauve cord inner soles, brown leather soles, signed "M.B. Paris" "1". 2 5/8" L. Circa 1885.

248. French Black Leather Shoes with Greyhound Insignia
Black leather shoes with ankle straps, gold button and button hole closures, brown overcast edging, brown silk ribbons, white card inners, dark brown soles, signed with insignia of greyhound, and "Paris P, "1". 2 3/8" L. Circa 1885.

249. French Black Leather Shoes for Rabery, Size 1
Black leather shoes with low-cut vamp and ankle straps with silver button closure, overcast brown edging, pink paper lining, brown taffeta bows, brown leather soles with incised outline, signed "Rabery Paris" and "1". 2 3/4" L. Circa 1885.

250. Black Leather Shoes with Brown Silk Rosettes
Black leather shoes have ankle straps with double silver button closure on black die-cut band, white over-stitching, brown silk rosette, mauve card lining, leather soles. 3" L. Circa 1885.

250A. Brown Leather Shoes with Maroon Trim Signed "Bebe le Parisien"0
Of polished brown leather, the slipper-style shoes have red overcast edging, maroon silk bows, brown leather soles with incised edging, marked "19" and "Bebe Le Parisien". 3 3/4" L. Circa 1885.

250B. Black Leather Shoes with "Passage des Panoramas" Label
Of irridescent black leather, the shoes have instep strap with silk rosette trim, high ankle strap with silk bow closure, additional silk rosette on vamp, brown leather soles, marked "Passage des Panoramas" and "Paris, L. de Pouy" 3"l. Circa 1885.

251. Green Velvet Frock with Juliette Sleeves
Of soft green velvet, the high-waist frock has fitted bodice with decorative gimp appliques, full gathered skirt, rounded neckline with self-banding, fitted coat sleeves whose upper halves are covered with very full puffed and gathered green velvet (the inside lining causing the upper sleeves to keep their puffed shape), gimp decorations on lower sleeves, hook and eye closures. 6 1/2" shoulder width. 20" bodice (underarm circumference). 19 1/2" overall length. Circa 1890.

252. Green Velvet Hat with Wide Brim
Flat-topped firm-sided green velvet hat has triple bands of rose satin and pale green velvet, wide brim with rose satin edging, decorated with feathers and silk bows; pale green velvet under-brim with rose silk bows and streamers, silk twill lining. To fit 7" head circumference. Circa 1895.

253. Green Velvet Capote Bonnet with Striped Silk Ribbons
Of rich green velvet the soft-crown bonnet with generous gathers, has wired brim, rose silk brim lining, stiffened net crown lining, striped silk ribbons and bands, maroon silk streamers. To fit 9" head circumference. Circa 1890.

254. Enameled Tole Faux Watch and Fob
The round pocket watch has faux-porcelain face with Roman numerals, movable hands, enclosed within floral-decorated tole case with green background, brass backing, attached to brass chain fob with fob decoration. Signed P.F. Paris. Circa 1890. 1 3/8" diam. watch.

255. Doll's Trousseau in Presentation Box
Arranged in original white satin-paper box with gold edging is a doll's trousseau comprising: oyster-white moire silk frock with dropped waist, box pleats, lantern sleeves, fitted cuffs, rich wool embroidery at the yoke, sash and skirt panels, rose satin bow at sash back; and dimity cotton pinafore with gathered bodice, lace and

tuck-trimmed yoke, long ties; and Charlotte silk bonnet with Alencon lace wide brim and rose satin bows, with matching ivory slippers with rose bows; and apron with drawnwork and tucking; and chemise and bloomers with fitted cuffs, and small ball-in-net toy. 3 1/2" shoulder width. 9" waist. 9" overall dress length. Circa 1885.

256. Flowered Voile
Dress with Green Velvet Trim
The two-piece dress has fitted bodice with rose muslin blouson bodice overlaid with open-weave lace, sheer flowered-voile bodice-back and sleeves, the bodice-back with gathers at shoulders and waist, inset waistband, puffed 3/4 length sleeves with green velvet cuffs and gimp trim, lace collar, green velvet faux-bolero front and epaulets trimmed with gimp, fully-lined bodice and sleeves. With matching flowered-voile skirt having inverted box pleats at front, gathers at back, set-in waistband, separate brown muslin underskirt. And matching black cummerbund trimmed with green silk folds. 5" shoulder width. 9 1/2" waist. 13" skirt length. Circa 1885.

257. White Leather Shoes with Stockings and Garters
Of soft kid leather with shapely wedge-shaped back, ankle straps with silver button and loop closure, white overcast edging, white card lining, leather soles with incised edging, signed "60". With open-work back-seamed lisle stockings and cord garters with rose silk bows. 2 3/4" L. Circa 1885.

91

258. Straw Hat with Upturned Side Brim in Original Box
Constructed of tightly-woven narrow bands of straw, with shallow flat crown, wide brims, one side brim turned up at 90 degree angle; decorated on top with embroidered lace and a border of ruched mousseline; on under brim with gathered mousseline and an ornate silk twill bow. Contained in original presentation with engraving on lid depicting the bonnet. To fit 8" head circumference. Circa 1885.

259. Straw Hat with Flat Crown and Large Roses
Of wide bands of loosely-woven straw with curled and crinkled tips and borders, the broad-brimmed hat has constructed back form overlaid with muslin and covered with a wall of over-sized flowers and leaves; the top of hat has band of bunched mousseline de soie and additional over-sized flowers. To fit 11" head circumference. Circa 1885.

260. Straw Pork-pie Hat with Silk Crown
Of unusual oyster-white-dyed woven straw, with soft flat crown of gathered mauve silk satin, and rounded straw brims, the hat is designed to perch atop the head in the manner of 1865-era fashion doll hats. Decorated on the outside with pleated ivory silk band and cluster of ivory mousseline with a centered monture of tiny white flowers; on the inside with a pleated border of mauve silk, pleated muslin lining. To fit 10" head circumference. Circa 1885.

261. Straw Hat with One-sided Upturned Brim
Of closely-woven bands of straw, with shallow flat-topped crown and very wide brim, one side brim pinned up and attached to crown, decorated with monture of cascading violets. Stamped "7" inside head. To fit 10" head circumference. Circa 1885.

262. Ivory Silk Satin Cabriolet Bonnet
Of fine ivory silk satin, padded and hand-quilted in small squares, the collapsible-

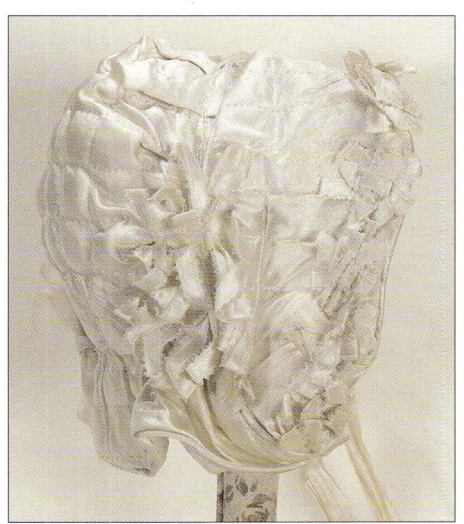
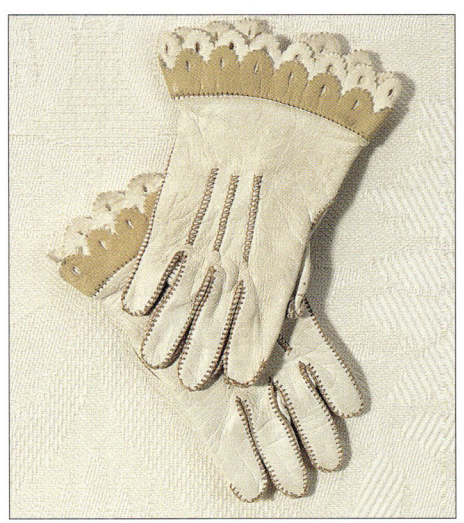

side bonnet has wide 2 1/2" brim, gathered bavolet with strings en coulisse for adjustable size, border of silk rosettes frames the face, silk ties. To fit 4 1/2" face width. Circa 1885.

263. White Leather Gloves with Tan Leather Edging
Short white leather wrist gloves have tan overcast stitching on fingers, separate thumb, decorative seams on top of hand, fitting slit with button and button holes, and two scalloped-edge borders (one of tan leather), 3" L. Circa 1885.

264. Purple Velvet Silver-Clasp Purse and Mauve Leather Gloves
The purse with silver clasp inscribed "Pat'd Feb 2 '75 (and indecipherable)", has leather interior, cotton twill sides with unusual printed pattern, and purple velvet sides, purple rope and tassels. With mauve leather gloves having overcast edges, separate thumb, three decorative seams, scalloped border. 3" W. purse. 4" L. gloves. Circa 1880.

265. Mauve Silk Faille Frock and Ivory Silk Faille Bonnet
Of vertically-ribbed mauve silk faille, the jacket-style frock with dropped waist has constructed bodice with goffered mousseline de soie plastron, and overlay jacket sides, rounded neckline with ivory silk banding, double-seam 3/4 length curved coat sleeves with lace-edged goffered mousseline de soie cuffs, flat front skirt panel, pleated sides and back of skirt, ivory satin hip bow, feather-stitched decoration on faux-lapels and sleeves, hook and eye closure. With soft-sided ivory twill Bibi Bonnet having five rows of ruching on side and top of very wide brim, lace rosette at crest topped with mousseline de soie, ivory silk cluster and cord tassels, lace edging, silk lining. 4 3/4" shoulder width. 16 1/2" hip width. 14" overall length. Cap to fit 12" head circumference. Circa 1882.

266. Cotton Voile Communion Ensemble with Accessories
The transparent, heavily sized, voile ensemble comprises blouse with narrow nun's tucks covering complete front and back, embroidered band collar, full sleeves with embroidered band cuffs and lace ruffle, three-button closure; and matching double-layered skirt with flat front panel and cartridge pleating at sides and back, waistband, hook and eye closure; and floor-length voile veil; and stiffened tulle coronet trimmed with gathered ruffle of tulle, ivory silk ties; and moire silk reticule with cord edging and handle; silk moire sash with large bow; white beaded rosary; and undergarments: pantalets, petticoat, chemise and full slip. 5" shoulder width. 10" waist. 10" skirt length. Circa 1890.

267. Blue Silk Faille Dress for Mignonette
Of blue silk faille with narrowest ribbing, the princess-style dress has lace-edged front opening (designed to be stitched closed), 3/4 length curved sleeves, Alencon lace trim at collar, cuffs, and skirt hem; black insertion lace at bottom of skirt through which is drawn blue velvet ribbon; blue satin bow at derriere. With matching black lace fanchon edged with blue velvet ribbons and trimmed with blue silk bows. 1 1/2" shoulder width. 4" dress length. Circa 1885.

268. Green Silk Faille Frock and Straw Duckbill Hat
Of bronze-green silk faille, the frock has fitted front and back yokes, gathered front and back bodice, lantern sleeves with wide cuff bands at the elbow trimmed with embroidered tulle, inset waistband, gathered skirt, peach silk satin semi-attached pleated sash with bow, fully lined, hook and eye closure. 4" shoulder width. 11 1/2" waist. 10 1/2" length. And duckbill hat constructed of braided straw in overlapping bands, with narrow brim at back and very wide brim at front, rounded shallow crow, the top of hat is decorated with five spider clusters of narrow rose silk ribbons, silk lining. To fit 8" head circumference. Circa 1885.

269. Two-Color Straw Bonnet with Straw "Feathers"
Entirely of woven straw bands and decorations, with rounded crown and slightly-sloping brim, the narrow bands of intricately-woven straw are decorated with a lavish band of straw curls and a straw "feather". To fit 8" head circumference. Circa 1880.

270. Aqua Silk and Cutwork Frock and Capote Bonnet
Aqua silk frock has rounded neck shaped by four rows of smocking above four centered box-pleats that taper toward the dropped waist and end with a narrow back of tight gathers at the hips; bordered by faux-jacket of elaborate re-embroidered cutwork through which the aqua silk under-dress is visible; with very short cotton-lined cutwork sleeves wider at the bottom than at the top, decorated with silk shoulder knots; aqua silk skirt of very narrow pleats is overlaid with a gathered skirt of re-embroidered white cutwork whose scalloped edge ends 1" higher than the underskirt. Trimmed with very wide draped aqua silk hip sash, large bows at each hip, two silk medallions and a monture of delicate flowers, hook and eye closure. With capote bonnet of Swiss muslin over aqua silk, wired ruffled aqua silk brim decorated on inside with pleated lace, and on outside with pleated lace and a monture of tiny flowers, silk streamers, tulle lining. 5" shoulder width. 18" hip width. 12 1/2" length. Circa 1882.

271. White Wool Challis and Aqua Silk Dress
The princess-style jacket dress has white wool challis jacket sides and back with vandyked tails, rounded neck whose inside is edged with aqua silk bordered with dentelled Alencon lace with exquisite embroidery detail, dart-shaped form-fitting wool challis jacket back, aqua silk plastron with smocking at the neckline and generous rouleaux at the hips (the plastron slightly padded for richer draping); double-seam curved coat sleeves with cuff edging of silk and lace to match the neckline; double-tiered box-pleated aqua silk satin skirt with balayeuse; the jacket is lined with soft cotton sateen, the skirt with buckram, hook and eye closure, decorative silver hook and eye at neckline. 7" shoulder width. 19" hip width. 16" length. Circa 1885.

272. Aqua Leather Shoes signed Bru Jne, Size 9, with Stockings
Aqua leather shoes are cut low with straps across the top of foot, silver buttons and loop closure, aqua overcast binding, aqua silk rosettes, twill lining, card inners, dark brown soles marked "Bru Jne/Paris" and "9". With matching lisle stockings having back seam, openwork at tops. 3" L. Circa 1885.

273. White Leather Shoes signed "A.T."
White leather shoes with overcast white binding, ankle straps with gold button and loop closure, ivory silk twill bows, brown card lining, dark brown soles marked "L'Excelsior A.T. Bebe Francais" and "11". 3 7/8" L. Circa 1885.

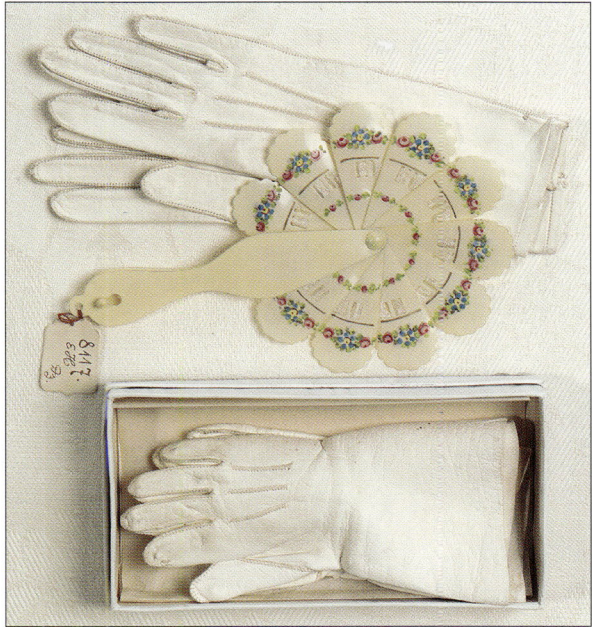

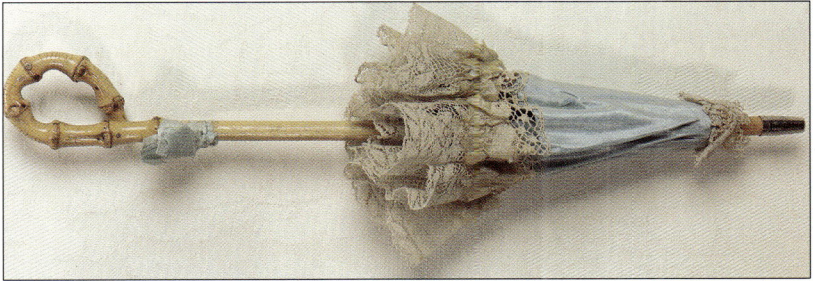

274. White Leather Shoes signed L.P. and Straw Leghorn Hat
White leather shoes have ankle straps with attached ties, overcast edging in slightly darker tones, ivory silk rosettes, card liners, leather soles signed L.P. 2 7/8" L. And woven straw leghorn-style hat with flat crown, wide flat brim, silk band, silk lining, tie cords. To fit 11" diam. head. Circa 1890.

275. Enameled Faux Watch and Brooch Pin
The faux watch has turquoise enamel with floral design on one side with ormulu grip, faux glass-fronted watch with Roman numerals on the reverse, attached to gilt ormulu brooch pin in the shape of bow. 7/8" diam. watch. Circa 1890.

276. Cardboard Folio "Bebe"
Cardboard folio with blue paper sides, gilt striping and gilt lettering "Bebe", has firm-sided base, and brown muslin sides, cord handles. 1 1/2 x 2 1/4". Circa 1885.

277. Blue Silk Satin Two-Piece Dress
The fitted blouse, of tulle overlaid on blue silk satin, has dart-shaping with tiny gathers at the center waist, notch cuts at the waist, rounded neckline with self-piping and lace fraise, double-seam curved coat sleeves with elbow shaping pleat, cuffs edged by double border lace centered with braided blue silk ribbons; sewn-down lace yoke, silk ribbon binding at bottom edges of blouse; hook and eye closure. And gored skirt with flat front panel, pleated back with center box pleat, narrow band of ivory silk ruching, net lining. 5" shoulder width. 12" waist. 14" skirt length. Circa 1882.

278. Maplewood-Handled Parasol with Blue Silk Cover
The maplewood handle with faux-bamboo turnings and curved shepherdess crook has metal tip, blue silk satin cover, eight prongs which open and close, two borders of openwork lace with center border of ivory silk ruche. 12 1/2" L. Circa 1890.

279. White Leather Gloves with Double Button Closure
Soft white leather gloves with overcast stitching at fingers and separate thumb, bound edge with finished slit and double buttons and button holes, three decorative seams on tops. 6 1/2" L. Circa 1895.

280. Celluloid Folding Fan
The ivory celluloid fan folds flat and closed, or opens to complete ten-blade circle which can be locked in place with hinging pin, decorated with floral design and interwoven ribbons, with original store label. 6" L. Circa 1895.

281. White Leather Elbow-Length Gloves in Original Box
Soft white leather gloves with over-cast stitching at fingers, and separate thumb, have cut-slit with overcast edging and button closure at the wrist, extended elbow length. In original glove box from Grand Magasins du Louvre. 5" L. Circa 1895.

282. Rose Silk Satin Frock and Woven Straw Hat
Of soft rose silk satin, the princess-style frock has full-length center panel of six pleats, hip-length faux-jacket whose sides are edged in dentelled embroidered lace, form-fitted pleated hip-length back bodice which falls freely onto back pleated skirt and is edged with self-banding and dentelled lace which continues around the front meeting the vertical bands of lace; lantern sleeves whose shape is held by fitted internal sleeves and wide snug sleeve band, lace trim at rounded neckline and sleeve bands, lining, hook and eye closure. And woven straw hat with ruffled brim pulled into a bunch at back of head, flat shallow crown, rose silk ribbon bands and bows, paper lining. 3 3/4" shoulder width. 14 1/2" hips. 10 1/2" length. Circa 1885.

283. Rose Silk Frock with Bertha Collar and Charlotte Bonnet
The rose silk satin frock has fitted bodice overlaid with wide Bertha collar that falls below the waistband, box-

pleated skirt, full 3/4 length sleeves, gathered self-ruffle at skirt hem, cotton guipure lace at collar edge, cuffs and skirt ruffle, lined, hook and eye closure. With Charlotte bonnet of rose silk overlaid with fine tulle, band of rose silk, rose floral decoration, braid edging, silk streamers. 3 1/2" shoulder width. 11 1/2" waist. 10 1/2" length. Circa 1890.

284. Rose Silk Satin Bodice
Of lustrous rose silk satin duchesse, the form-fitting bodice has round neckline edged with ruched mousseline de soie, V-shaped bands of mousseline edging a lace overlay at center of front bodice, 3/4 length full sleeves drawn together by box pleats at the elbow band and decorated with ruched mousseline border and lace, button closure. 6" shoulder width. 18" waist. Circa 1885.

285. Wooden-Handled Parasol with Striped Silk Cover
Simple wooden handle with embossed metal cap and tassel and cord trim, has six prongs, opens and closes, original rose striped cover and scalloped-edge lace border. 11" L. Circa 1890.

286. Rose Satin Dress with Bertha Collar and Matching Hat
Of fine rose silk satin with interwoven tiny pattern, the dress has yoke of very narrow pleats below a band collar with embroidered lace overlay, wide lace-edged ruffled Bertha collar which extends around both front and back bodice, dropped waist, blouson bodice constructed of four sets of narrow pleats alternating with lace-over-silk panels; box-pleated skirt, lantern sleeves with fitted interior sleeves and snug wide lace-trimmed bands, rose satin sash and bow. And matching flat-brimmed hat with very wide wire-shaped brim, lace-covered on top, ribbon band and large bow, silk rose petals, underside edged in point d'esprit, cord ties. 4 1/2" shoulder width. 14" hip width. 12" length. Circa 1885.

287. Straw Lamballe Bonnet
Of tightly woven very narrow bands of straw, the shallow crown is flat-topped with center indentation, wide brim is shaped to fold under at front and back creating a straight line edge; the outside is decorated with monture of white flowers and generous cluster of rose velvet narrow ribbons; the inside has similar decorations, muslin lining, velvet streamers. To fit 13" width head. Circa 1885.

288. Black Leather Shoes by Alart, Size 10
Of black leather with pointy toes, ankle straps with double button and loop closure, black silk rosettes, white card inners, unusual black leather soles impressed with figure of doll in chemise and "Depose" and "10". 3 1/2" L. Circa 1890.

289. Black Leather Shoes by Alart, Size 11
Black leather shoes with very wide ankle straps, brown overcast edging, double pair of lacing holes with brown grosgrain laces, metal tips, brown silk rosettes, twill lining, cord inners, dark brown leather soles marked with figure of doll in chemise and "A La Providence/74 rue de Rivoli" and "11". 3 7/8" L. Circa 1890.

290. Stiffened Lace Leghorn Hat
Of loosely-woven bands of heavily-stiffened lace, the shallow-flat-topped hat has very wide brim with outside border of woven curly straw, band of bunch rose crepe silk. To fit 9 1/2" head circumference. Circa 1895.

291. Blue Cotton Sateen Frock and Wire-Framed Bonnet
Of shadow-woven blue cotton sateen, the frock has simple form-fitting lines with defined waist, band neckline with lace overlay, wide lace Bertha collar that defines the bodice, two box pleats down full front of dress, 3/4 length full sleeves,

lace-edged sleeve bands, narrow blue silk ribbon rosettes at neckline, blue silk ribbon ties at back, neck lining. With matching Charlotte bonnet having soft blue silk crown, with blue silk ribbon bands and bows, wire-framed very wide brim covered with mousseline de soie. 4" shoulder width. 12 1/2" hip width. 11 1/2" length. Circa 1890.

292. Woven Metallic-Thread Fedora
Metallic threads are woven in straw-like bands and arranged on a wire armature with rounded crown, brim that appears narrow on the exterior and wide on the interior, wound ivory silk band terminating in large back-of-head rosette of ivory silk and metallic ribbon, two borders of Alencon lace at edge of brim, silk lining, cord tie. To fit 9" head circumference. Circa 1890.

293. Aqua Cotton Sateen Blouson Frock with Bretelles
Of lustrous aqua cotton sateen printed with darker turquoise dots, the one-piece frock has fitted muslin under bodice, blouson sateen front and back bodice, fitted front and back yokes with hand-made cotton lace overlay bordered by three narrow bands of sateen, 3/4 length full sleeves whose tops are hidden under extended bretelles, inset waistband, three-panel flared skirt with three rows of tucking and one row of ruffles at the hem, fully lined, hook and eye closure. Trimmed with gimp and aqua silk satin bow. 5" shoulder width. 13 1/2" waist. 13" full length. Circa 1890.

294. Blue Cotton Sateen Frock with Bertha Collar
Of pale blue lustrous cotton sateen, the one-piece frock has fitted bodice with blouson bodice below tiny narrow sewn-down tucks, V-shaped tucks at back, 3/4 length full sleeves with set-in cuff bands, gore-shaped skirt with sewn-down darts and gusset-shaping, three bands of tucks at hemline, muslin-lined bodice, hook and eye closure, blue satin sash with silver mount. With matching detachable Bertha collar having tatted lace insertsand edging. 4 1/2" shoulder width. 12" waist. 15" overall Circa 1890.

295. Black Leather Shoes by Alart, Size 12
Shiny black leather shoes with pointy tips, tiny border of holes around front through which hosiery color could peek, ankle straps with lacing holes, black silk laces, cord inners, brown leather soles signed with figure of doll in chemise and "Depose" and "12". 4 1/8" L. Circa 1890.

296. Rose Cotton Voile Frock with Bertha Collar
Of soft rose cotton voile printed with same-color tiny flowers, the frock has fitted bodice with gathered center panel, round banded neckline, inset yoke with lace overlay, two lace bands edging the center panel, wide ruffled Bertha collar with 1" lace border, 3/4" length full sleeves with lace-trimmed bands and long lace ruffles, full skirt of narrow knife pleats with 2" lace trim near the hemline, lined bodice, hook and eye. 5" shoulder width. 13" waist. 16" length. Circa 1895.

297. Ivory Silk Frock with Double Lace Collars
Of very delicate ivory silk woven with tiny dots, the frock has fitted bodice with wide center panel of generous narrow pleats, round collar with lace overlay interwoven with rose silk ribbons, two wide ruffled collars that extend around the entire neckline, lantern sleeves with interior form-fitted shape, sleeve bands overlaid with rose-ribbon beaded lace, long lace sleeve ruffles, inset waistband overlaid with lace woven with rose silk ribbons, pleated full skirt with five rows of wide tucks, lined bodice, buttons and loops. 6" shoulder width. 17 1/2" waist. 16" length. Circa 1895.

298. Straw Bonnet with Rose Petals
The bonnet cap, designed to closely hug the head is constructed of wide bands of braided straw, edged with two bands of scalloped Valenciennes ruffled lace and band of ruched silk ribbon, long silk streamers, montures of tiny rose petals at each front corner and rosette of ivory grosgrain ribbon, long silk streamers, shaped organdy lining. To fit 16" head circumference. Circa 1885.

299. Pale Rose Silk Charlotte Bonnet
Of very delicate rose silk printed with tiny flowers, the beret-shaped soft crown is edged with two wide wire-shaped brims, one with vandyked edge, the other with stiffened embroidered tulleborder, and a band of arranged moire silk ribbon with three moire bows, cord ties. To fit 12" head circumference. Circa 1890.

299A. Black Leather Shoes Signed "B" for Bru, Size 6
Of soft black leather with muslin lining, brown silk edging, ankle straps, black button and loop closures, black rosettes and silver buckles, brown leather soles, signed "B" in script and 6. 2 3/4" L. Circa 1883

299B. Black Leather Shoes Signed "B" for Bru, Size 4
Of soft black leather with muslin lining, brown silk edging, ankle straps, double black button and loop closures, black rosettes and silver buckles, brown leather soles, signed "B" in script and 4. 2 1/4" L. Circa 1883

300. Rose Silk Dress and Matching Bonnet
Of lightweight rose silk, the dress has low-rounded collar, dropped waist, sewn-down tucks of graduated length at yoke, box-pleated skirt, short sleeves, hand-made tatting trim at neckline, cuffs, along the shoulders, and skirt, band of drawnwork at hips, button closure. With matching wire-framed bonnet. 3 1/2" shoulder width. 12 1/2" hip width. 9 1/2" dress length. Circa 1895.

301. Maroon Leather Shoes Signed with Boot Symbol
Soft maroon leather shoes have ankle straps with brass grommets and silk lacing ribbon, leather soles marked with insignia of boot and "Depose", "2". 1 3/4" L. Circa 1890.

**302. Black Leather Shoes
*with Script Letter Signature***
Of soft black leather with overcast stitching, ankle straps with double brown silk button and loop closure, brown silk rosettes with silk button center, white card inners, yellow leather soles marked with script letters and "2". 1 1/2" L. Circa 1885.

303. Rose Silk Satin and Mousseline Frock and Hat
The two-piece frock has rose silk satin fitted bodice with box-pleated peplum, ruched mousseline plastron edged with gathered ribbons and wide ruffled mousseline bretelles also edged with gathered ribbons, rounded neckline edged with Valenciennes lace and beading lace with silk ribbons, puffed mousseline sleeves over silk satin, wide fitted cuffs tied with silk ribbons and mousseline ruche, ribbon-trimmed mousseline bretelles extend down the back bodice, rose satin pleated sash with large bow, fully lined, hook and eye closure. With matching three-panel flared skirt slightly gathered in the back, trimmed with mousseline ruche. And wire-framed hat with very wide ruffled mousseline front brim, ruffled beret-style crown trimmed with bows, buckram lining, cord ties. 3 1/2" shoulder width. 12" waist. 5" skirt length. Circa 1890.

304. Rose Cotton Sateen Frock, Bonnet and Undergarments
Of rose cotton sateen with delicately-woven floral-shadow pattern, the frock has richly-gathered yoke bordered by self-banded round neckline and a variation of the Bertha collar (having six separate panels that extend around to the back over a wide embroidered tulle collar and which hides the blouson bodice). Full-length double-seam coat sleeves with lace cuffs, lightly-gathered skirt, rose silk sash which matches bonnet sash, muslin lining, extra built-in petticoat, hook and eye closures. With matching capote bonnet with soft crown, wired ruffled brim, silk bows and streamers, buckram lining. With matching lace-edged chemise and two draw-string petticoats. 4" shoulder width. 11" waist. 11" length. Circa 1890.

305. Black Leather Shoes signed with Hot Air Balloon
Black leather shoes have ankle straps with button and hole closure, black overcast edging, very large black silk rosettes, cardboard inners, tan soles with incised outline, symbol of hot air balloon and "Marque Depose" and "10". 3 1/2" L. Circa 1885.

306. Black Leather Shoes signed A.T.
Of soft black leather with ankle straps having silver button and loop closure, brown silk rosettes with silver medallions, white card inners, leather soles signed "A.T." and "6". 2 3/8" L. Circa 1885.

307. Black Leather Shoes Signed Eden Bebe
Black leather shoes with brown overcast edges, ankle straps with silver button and hole closure, purple card inners, brown leather soles signed "Eden Bebe Paris" and "6". 2 1/4" L. Circa 1890.

308. Peach Mousseline de Soie Bonnet Cap
The soft cap is constructed of buckram overlaid with silk satin and, again, overlaid with generously-ruched bands of mousseline de soie, embroidered back-of-head circlet, wire-framed brim with clusters of mousseline and silk ribbon rosettes, lace bavolet, silk streamers. To fit 15 - 15 1/2" head circumference. Circa 1885.

309. Challis Wool Frock with
Dimity Collar and Cloche Straw Hat
Of fine oyster-white challis wool, the high-waisted frock has fitted front and back bodice, rounded neckline with large dimity Pilgrim collar edged in fine tatting, narrow inset panel at center of bodice overlaid with the same tatting and three rosette-trimmed bands of ivory silk, full-length full sleeves with wide fitted cuffs under dimity cuffs with tatted edging. Four-fold pleated sash with long self-ties, passementerie trim, silk bows. Three-panel flared skirt with row of tatting at hemline, full bodice lining, hook and eye closure. With straw cloche having rounded crown and wide sloping brim, overlaid with Alencon lace, wound velvet band and edging, fabric flowers and leaves, silk lining, (illegible) label. 6 1/2" shoulder width. 18" high waist. 18" dress length. Fits 14" head circ. Circa 1890.

310. Magenta Silk Parasol in Original Box
With wooden handle having curved hand clasp painted red with floral design, and metal tips, the six-pronged parasol which opens and closes has original magenta silk cover with scalloped edging, inset band of tulle lace, and is contained in original maroon box labelled "Ombrella pour Poupee/article en satinet dentelle". 13 1/2" L. Circa 1895.

311. Wool Challis Gretchen Dress with Rubens Straw Bonnet
Of fine oyster-white challis wool the dress has self-banded round collar with feather-stitching, fitted front and back yoke with narrow rows of tucking and embroidery, very wide Bertha collar with embroidered scalloped edging and embroidery, wide box pleats that fall freely from the yoke, inverted box pleat at center front, 3/4 length gathered sleeves with smocking and ruffles at the cuffs, light flannel lining, button closure. With flat-topped straw bonnet having flat brim, decorated on top with wound velvet maroon ribbon and maroon boa; maroon velvet lines the underside of brim, silk lining, cord ties. 7" shoulder width. 21 1/2 underarm circumference. 15" dress length. To fit 14" head circumference. Circa 1885.

312. Astrakan Cap, Collar and Muff
Of fleecy white astrakan, the set comprises toque with silk lining, silk-lined collar with silver buckles at neckline, and silk-lined muff with silk cord ties. To fit 11 1/2" head circumference. Circa 1890.

313. White Leather Boots with Red Trim
Ankle boots of white leather are bound with overcast red thread, have lacing holes around the ankle allowing red velvet ribbon to show at the sides of foot, and red pom-pom trim, leather soles signed "6". 2 7/8" L. Circa 1890.

314. Rose Cotton Sateen Wooden-Handled Umbrella
With maplewood handle having curved hand-clasp and silver tip, the seven-pronged umbrella opens and closes, has red pom-pom and tassel trim, and is contained in original maroon paper box with gold edging. 14 1/2" L. Circa 1890.

Chapter VI

Pinafores and Aprons
1865 - 1910

316. Brown Muslin Pinafore with Scalloped Cotton Trim
Of lightweight very-tightly-woven brown muslin, the dress has square-edged neckline with self-banding pleated at the corners, eight loose box pleats down the entire length of front held by stitched-down 4" waist band that evolves into long loose ties, mancheron sleeves wider at the top and with open-slits at top, two pockets, three rows of narrow hem tucks, open back; the neckline, sleeves, waistband and pockets with scallop-edged broderie Anglaise. 3 1/2" shoulder width. Circa 1865.

317. Natural Linen Long-Sleeved Smock Dress
Of finely-woven natural linen, the smock has double-thickness fitted front and back yoke with narrow white cording at rounded neckline and bodice edge, three full-length box pleats from the yoke, slightly-full long sleeves with fitted cuffs embroidered with light feather stitch, gusset underarms, gathered free-falling back, belt loops, maroon silk satin sash, buttons and button holes at back yoke and cuffs. 6 1/2" shoulder width. Circa 1870.

318. Blue and White Muslin Long-Sleeved Smock Dress
Of fine tightly-woven blue and white checkered muslin, the smock dress has double-thickness fitted front and back yoke edged with self-band at neckline trimmed with narrow

315. White Muslin Smock
Of fine quality white muslin, having low rounded neckline edged with narrow braid and ruffled broderie Anglaise, form-fitted upper bodice evolving into flared sides; bodice trimmed with drawn-work, tucks and feather-stitching, creating gathers below, open back with strings en coulisse closure at neckline, three rows of tucks and wide band of scalloped-edge broderie Anglaise at hip-length hemline, gigot sleeve with cartridge gathers at shoulders and cuffs, inset pleat at back side seam, fitted cuffs with four rows of tiny tucks, braid and broderie Anglaise, long tie backs. 5 1/2" shoulder width. Circa 1865.

white flat braid, three rows of white flat braid at bottom edge of V-shaped yoke, cartridge-pleated free-falling skirt, full sleeves with fitted cuffs, V-shaped pockets, three rows of white flat braid on cuffs, pockets and hemline; button and loop closures at back yoke and cuffs. 7" shoulder width. 18" length. Circa 1870.

319. Blue and White Chambray Hip-Length Smock Dress
Of sturdy tightly-woven blue and white checkered chambray, the smock dress has low-rounded collar with self-band above a row of Toby frills, six constructed bodice pleats that reverse direction at center, eight very narrow pleats clustered at center of back bodice, inset waistband, gathered hip-length skirt, 3/4 length slightly-gathered sleeves with cuffs, two bellows pockets with unusual band of narrow box pleats at edge suggesting that the pockets are double-layered; button and loop closures at neck, waist and cuffs. 6 1/2" shoulder width. 11" length. Circa 1870.

320. White Cambric Pinafore with Blue Cross-Stitch
White cambric with woven shadow-stripe, the sleeveless pinafore has fitted front and back bodice with banded narrow yoke, shoulder straps, three stitched-down box pleats at front and back bodice, cartridge-pleated skirt, four button and loop closure, elaborate blue-cross-stitch embroidery. 5 1/2" shoulder width. 15" waist. Circa 1880.

321. Pale Blue Muslin Smock
Of sturdy pale blue muslin, the princess-styled hip-length smock has low rounded neckline edged in flat white cord twill, 3/4 length sleeves with cuffs, attached back-belt at sides of waist, two V-shaped pockets, white cord twill at hemline. There are three rows of narrow white cord trim at neckline, cuffs, belts, pockets and hemline, button and loop closure. 6" shoulder width. 10 1/2" length. Circa 1875.

322. Linen Pinafore with Handmade Scalloped Embroidery
Of natural linen, the princess-style pinafore has rounded neckline with self-banding, mancheron sleeves, open back with long self-ties, and is decorated at neckline, sleeves, front panels and around the hemline with handmade scalloped-edge embroidery in red and blue. 5" shoulder width. 5" skirt length. Circa 1875.

323. Red Checkered Pinafore-Apron with Bretelle Collar
Of tiny red and white gingham checks, the pinafore apron has narrow bib-front constructed of V-shaped pleats that meet in the center, and which button-attach to bretelles that form a wide collar at the back, inset waistband with button closure, gathered skirt with bellow-shaped pockets, muslin-woven edging trim. 11 1/2" waist. 13" skirt length. Circa 1875.

324. Blue Checkered Pinafore-Apron with Soutache Trim
Of tiny blue and white gingham checks, the pinafore-apron has bib-front which pin-attaches to dress bodice, inset waistband with tie-backs, flat-front apron with two large pockets. The edges are scalloped indigo muslin with elaborate soutache embroidery in bow and loop design, and soutache outlines the pockets and blue pocket bands. 10" waist. 12" length. Circa 1875.

325. Ivory Cotton Sateen Pinafore Dress
Of fine cotton sateen with woven ribbed design, the pinafore dress has square-cut neckline, mancheron sleeves, fitted bodice, cartridge-pleated skirt, tacked-on self belt with long ties, button back bodice, open skirt-back, two V-shaped pockets, bands of muslin edging with scalloped borders and brown embroidered stars at hemline, sleeves, neck, pocket edges and as bretelles which frame the front tucked bodice. 5 1/2" shoulder width. 15 1/2" waist. 14" length. Circa 1880.

326. Red Muslin Pinafore Smock
With square-cut neckline and very high fitted yoke which is hidden under scalloped-edged cutwork collar, self-banded neckline, very full artist's sleeves with gathered cuffs, inset cuff band with buttoned closure, free-falling gathers from yoke, two pockets with embroidered cutwork, button back yoke, open back. The pinafore is trimmed with white embroidered cutwork. 5 1/4" shoulder width. 13" length. Circa 1875.

327. Red Muslin Pinafore
Princess-style pinafore has rounded neckline with hand-made rick-rack edging, mancheron sleeves, pockets and hemline with embroidered scalloped edging, cutwork and embroidered white flowers, two buttons at back top, long ties. 4 1/2" shoulder width. 9 1/2" length. Circa 1880.

328. Red Nainsook Pinafore Dress
Of tightly-woven red cotton, the pinafore dress has rounded neckline, three box pleats fall the entire front length of dress, one box pleat on either side of open back with four button top closure, long self ties, long cuffed sleeves. The dress is trimmed with three narrow bands of flat cord at neckline, cuffs, front waist and hemline. 5" shoulder width. 12" waist. 9 1/2" length. Circa 1880.

329. Red Nainsook Pinafore Dress with Bertha Collar
Of tightly-woven red cotton, the pinafore dress has rounded tight neckline with self-banding, mancheron sleeves gathered at top, fitted yoke above a wide ruffled Bertha collar that extends around the entire back, a series of narrow pleats begin under the Bertha collar and extend the full front and back length, two-button closure at top back, attached sash with button back. The pinafore is trimmed with three rows of white cord at collar, sleeves and hemline, and a looped cord design on yoke. 5 1/4" shoulder width. 14" waist. 14" length. Circa 1885.

330. Red Nainsook Pinafore Dress with Bertha Collar
Of identical fabric to #329, but having ruffled Bertha collar directly attached to V-shaped neckline and hiding the fitted yoke from which fall five narrow pleats, even narrow pleats under back Bertha collar, mancheron sleeves, attached sash with button and loop closure, three bands of narrow white cord trim the collar, sleeves and hem, single band outlines the neckline. 5 1/2" shoulder width. 13" length. 14" waist. Circa 1885.

331. Pair, White Cotton Twill Pinafores
Of ribbed white cotton twill, the princess-style pinafores have rounded necklines, capelet sleeves, two V-shaped pockets, button closure at top back, embroidered with tiny red cross-stitches. 5 1/2" shoulder width. 13" length. Circa 1880.

332. Cotton Muslin Skirt with Printed Panels
With inset waistband, the gathered skirt is of narrow red and white stripes with diamond blocks, has woven border with pattern of children playing with ball and loop toys. Hook and eye closure. 12 1/2" waist. 13 1/2" length. Circa 1885.

333. White Nainsook Pinafore Dress with Red Trim
With rounded neckline trimmed with ruffled collar having scalloped edge embroidered in red threads, cutwork and leaf pattern, mancheron sleeves constructed the same as collar, cartridge pleats at center front bodice creating fullness, gathered skirt, button back. 4 1/4" shoulder width. 13" waist. 10" length. Circa 1885.

334. White Cotton Pinafore
Of fine white ribbed cotton, with square-cut neckline, cutwork yoke and shoulder bands, ruffled capelet sleeves with cutwork edging, gathered free-falling front and back, self-ties, two pockets with cutwork edging, two buttons at back yoke. 3 1/2" shoulder width. 9 1/2" length. Circa 1885.

335. Mauve Printed Cotton Pinafore
Of white cotton printed with mauve pattern, the simple pinafore has square-cut neckline constructed of 1 1/2" yoke and shoulder bands that criss-cross each other, free-falling gathers from yoke band, graduated-width ruffled capelet sleeves with cotton lace trim, two buttons at back yoke. 6" shoulder width. 13" length. Circa 1885.

336. Printed Cotton Pinafore with Batiste Sleeves
Of printed cotton in rose colors and slight raised designs, the pinafore-frock has square-cut neckline constructed of 1 1/2" yoke and shoulder bands that criss-cross each other and are trimmed with narrower bands of cutwork, white batiste cotton ruffled capelet sleeves with scalloped diamond edging, free-falling gathers from yoke band, two pockets trimmed with drawnwork, long tie sash, handkerchief. 4 3/4" shoulder width. 13 1/2" length. Circa 1885.

337. Four-Piece White Cotton Ensemble with Pinafore
The ensemble comprises fine batiste white dress with rounded neckline edged in Swiss embroidery, ruffled Bertha collar edged in broderie Anglaise, fitted bodice with front and back narrow tucks and center band of cutwork, long fitted sleeves with turn-up cuffs, inset waistband, gathered skirt with elaborate band of cutwork and embroidery; and white muslin full slip with inset waistband, tucks and embroidery; and white Charlotte bonnet with double ruffled cutwork brims and crocheted crown, twill brim lining, rose silk band; and ribbed Swiss cotton apron with bib-front and narrow bretelles that extend around the head forming a back collar, inset waistband with long ties, two bellows pockets, handmade crocheted edging on bretelles and hemline. 5" shoulder width. 16" waist. 15" length. Circa 1885.

338. Muslin Bertha Collar in Original Box
With tarlatan cotton yoke having fitted round beading collar with rose silk ribbon, and bottom edging of same ribbon beading, pleated muslin Bertha collar with tatted edging. In original rose-paper lined box with pink bordered exterior and engraving of baby with rose ribboned gown. 3" neck circumference. Circa 1885.

Chapter VII

Dresses and Playsets
1890 - 1925

339. Navy Blue Jersey Two-Piece Ensemble
Of tightly-woven navy blue jersey, the ensemble comprises jacket-style top with hidden hook and eye closure at front under braid trim and edged by three vertical bands of self-piping, long sleeves with braid trim, rounded fold-down collar with braid trim; with matching flared skirt having sewn-down tucks 3/4 the length of the skirt, hook and eye closure. With sewn-in tag "10" indicating its production for size 10 Bebe Jumeau, as presented in Paris department store catalogues. 6" shoulder width. 12" waist. 9" skirt length. Circa 1900.

340. Two Pairs of Little/Big Sister Hats
Each with soft crown and wide firm brim, comprising pair in pale aqua cotton sateen with black velvet ribbon trim, floral decoration; and pair in black silk satin with ruffled upper brims, floral trim. Each pair, 3" and 4" inside brims. Circa 1915.

341. Pair, Blue Silk Doll Shoes
Of soft pale silk, the shoes have cream overcast edging, blue thread-covered buttons, pompoms, brown leather soles signed "3". 2 1/2" L. Circa 1910.

342. Pale Blue Kid Leather Shoes
Of soft blue kid leather with scalloped edge at lacing slit, three pairs of lacing grommets, leather soles, signed "7". 3 1/4" L. Circa 1910.

343. Pale Green Silk Satin Frock
Of lustrous soft pale green silk satin the one-piece frock has faux-tunic top that falls loosely to below the hips, centered front cording decorated with two clusters of self-covered buttons, cording around the neckline, 3/4 length sleeves with cording, buttons and lace cuffs, the tunic gathered into gathers at the sides and edged by self-sash at the back with tassel trim, lace collar with front and back diamond points trimmed with self-covered buttons, hook and eye closure. 5 1/2" shoulder width. 13" length. Circa 1915.

344. Aqua Cotton Sateen Twill Bonnet
In richly-ribbed aqua twill sateen, the bonnet has soft gathered back with dark green velvet medallion center and tatted border, ruffled brim of graduated width, buckram and silk lining, silk streamers, twill bows with green velvet cording at crest. To fit 3 1/2" facial width. Circa 1895.

345. Woven Straw Bonnet
Of loosely-woven intricate pattern, the straw in wide and very narrow widths, having scalloped brim, soft crown, aqua silk ribbons and banding, tissue lining. 2" head width. Circa 1895.

346. Aqua Silk Hat with Lace Ruffles
Muslin-framed bonnet has wide aqua silk-covered brim, soft crown, lavish covering of triple rows of ruffled scalloped lace, four tiers of lace on crown, green patterned silk brim and bow, small boa feather. Under brim has lace cover, green silk bows, muslin lining. 2" head width. Circa 1900.

347. Woven Straw Bonnet and Wooden-Handled Parasol
Of woven braided straw with straw cording, gathered construction of straw brim, flattened top, black velvet ribbons, chiffon bows, green plush berries, inside pleated silk lining. 2 1/2" head width. And wooden-handled parasol, with eight metal prongs that allows parasol to open and close, cotton cover with tiny floral print, brass ring belt loop. 15" L. Circa 1900.

348. Red Wool Flannel Frock with Bertha Collar
Of coarsely-woven red wool flannel, the drop-waist frock has blouson bodice shaped by narrow pleats at the fitted yoke, above a fitted muslin underblouse, 3/4 length sleeves with narrow pleats at shoulders and wrists, fitted wide-band cuffs, full skirt with narrow pleats, muslin skirt lining, attached wide Bertha collar with long red fringe and white embroidered checks, hook and eye closure. 4" shoulder width. 12" hips. 12" length. Circa 1910.

349. Maroon Wool Twill Frock
Of lightweight maroon wool twill, the one-piece frock has V-shaped pleats at fitted front and back bodice, fitted yoke overlaid with openwork heavy cotton lace, banded neckline, full-length sleeves with fullness at top narrowing to fitted darts at wrists and decorated with three buttons/button loops and featherstitching, three rows of tucks at the hemline of full skirt, hook and eye closure, muslin-lined bodice. 4" shoulder width. 12" waist. 11" length. Circa 1885.

350. Cream Mohair Plush Cloche
Mohair plush cloche has unstructured soft crown held by ivory silk banding and embroidery, silk lining, silk ties, lace edging. 7" head width. Circa 1915.

351. Cream Flannel Booties with Fleeced Lining
Cream wool flannel booties have lambswool fleeced interiors, one pair of metal-edged lacing grommets with laces, cotton pompoms, leather soles signed "4". 2 1/4" L. Circa 1915.

352. Crimson Silk Brocade and Velvet Frock with Matching Bonnet
Of crimson silk with patterned brocade design, the frock has muslin-lined fitted bodice with center-gathers, wide puffed sleeves with extended-length openwork lace edging, openwork lace yoke, very wide lace Bertha collar, rose velvet vertical band on skirt and collar decorations. With matching wire-framed velvet bonnet with graduated-width brim trimmed with cotton lace, red silk bow. 4 1/2" shoulder width. 12" waist. 14" length. Circa 1915.

353. Red Challis Polka Dot Dress with Bertha Collar
Of red lightweight challis with printed white polka dots, the dress has constructed fully-lined yoke above basted-down pleats that fall to 2" above the hem, long coat sleeves with basted-down pleats at the shoulders, set-in buttoned-cuffs, rows of vertical tucks, button back, very wide Bertha collar of embroidered white cotton and tatting. 6" shoulder width. 13" length. Circa 1910.

354. Red Cotton Polka Dot Dress with Cutwork Collar and Cuffs
Of red cotton with white polka dots, fitted yoke above simple gathered skirt, 3/4 length very full gathered sleeves, cream muslin collar and cuffs with embroidered cutwork, button and button hole closure. 4" shoulder width. 10" length. Circa 1910.

355. Pair, Cream Kid Leather Shoes
Of soft cream kid the shoes have cream overcast stitching on edges, three pairs of lacing holes, decorative stitching around edges, leather soles, original laces, signed "11" and remnants of original store label. 3 1/2" L. Circa 1915.

119

356. Yellow Plaid Cotton Flannel Frock
Of yellow plaid with narrow striped design of darker yellow and taupe. the high-waisted frock has fitted bodice over full gathered skirt, elbow-length puffed sleeves, rounded collar, button closure, front and back Bertha collar with very widely-extended wings over the sleeves, stitched-down yellow silk banding and ribbons on collars and sleeves. 4" shoulder width. 12" waist. 11" length. Circa 1910.

357. Cotton Lace Frock with Bertha Collar
Of openwork cotton lace with pale yellow under-dress, the dropped waist frock has blouson top, fitted tulle yoke, pagoda-shaped sleeves with lace-edging, two-tiered lace skirt, lace collar, wide Bertha collar with three bands of yellow ribbons, ruffled lace edging, button closure. 5" shoulder width. 13" hips. 12" overall length. Circa 1915.

358. White Cotton Dropped Waist Frock and Slip
White finely-woven cotton frock has slightly dropped waist with narrow sewn-down tucks at shoulders, set-in center panel with alternating bands of pale yellow silk ribbons and lace edged by vertical lace bands, lace and cotton "wings" at bodice, 3/4 length sleeves with fitted cuffs, gathered skirt beginning at sides of center panel, gathered hem ruffles, pale yellow ribbon trim, button closure. Included is white cotton slip with cutwork trim. 8" shoulder width. 20" dropped waist. 18" length. Circa 1910.

359. Rose Chambray Cotton Frock
Rose chambray frock has fitted yoke decorated with V-shaped bands of cutwork and embroidery, ruffled lace collar, full gathered sleeves with lace edging, featherstitched decoration on skirt band, full gathered skirt with insertion cutwork band near the hem, button closure. 4" shoulder width. 11" length. Circa 1910.

360. Pin-Striped Rose Cotton Frock with Floral Design
Of fine rose cotton sateen with woven pin stripes and decorative roses and leaves, the frock has high fitted yoke above a full skirt with double pleats on either side of central box pleat, very full bishop sleeves with gathering at elbows, lace trim at collar, button closure. 3" shoulder width. 12" length. Circa 1910.

361. White Cotton Pique Frock with Lace Bonnet and Leather Shoes
White pique frock has slightly dropped waist with full gathered bodice and skirt, lined fitted yoke with applied cutwork trim, 3/4 length full sleeves with set-in cuffs, wide ruffled Bertha collar with cutwork embroidered border, hook and eye closure. 4" shoulder width. 13" dropped waist. 10" length. With pale green kid leather boots having four-button closure, leather soles, black heels. And wire-framed cloche overlaid with fine muslin and toucle tiers of fine starched lace, monture of white flowers, rose muslin lining. Circa 1915.

362. White Batiste Frock with Matching Undergarments, Shoes, Socks
Sheer white cotton batiste frock has dropped waist with loosely-fitted bodice, vertical bands of lace on bodice, lace at hips with insertion ribbon for fitting, gathered skirt with three rows of lace, 3/4 length sleeves with double rows of lace and insertion ribbon. With matching slip, pantalets, petticoat, rose silk stockings, leather shoes with rose silk ribbons (signed 5). 5" shoulder width. 15" hip width. 14" length. Circa 1915.

363. Two Pairs of Rose Shoes
Comprising cotton twill shoes with silver buckle trim, leather soles, and matching openwork stockings, 3 1/4" L. And rose leather shoes with silver buckles, ankle straps with button closure, leather soles, 1 3/4" L. Circa 1900.

364. Pale Blue Gingham Frock and Sunbonnet
Of sturdy blue cotton gingham, the dress has set-in yoke, tightly-gathered bodice, gathered skirt, wide bretelles over Juliette sleeves with full gathers at top of arms, tightly-fitted sleeves from above the elbows, ruffled white cotton collar and cuffs, appliqued bands of cutwork at bodice, waist, sleeves, and bretelles. With matching sunbonnet with wide brim, adjustable pull-strings in casing, ties, cutwork edging. 5 1/2" shoulder width. 13" waist. 14" overall. Circa 1910.

365. Pale Blue/Cream Cotton Print Frock
Pale cream frock with blue printed flowers and abstract design, has fitted bodice with vertical tucks, narrow cotton lace Bertha collar, cotton lace neckline and waist-trim, 3/4 length gathered sleeves with lace trim, gathered skirt with two rows of horizontal tucks at the hemline, button back. 4 1/2" shoulder width. 10" waist. 12" length. Circa 1910.

366. Cream Matelasse Cotton Frock and Batiste Cap
Of embossed-woven-pattern in cream cotton printed with delicate sprigs of blue and rose flowers and leaves, the frock has high fitted yoke overlaid with lace, self-rounded collar, pleats falling the entire length of dress from yoke with inverted pleats at center and back, full gathered sleeves, hook and eye closure. With matching batiste ruffled Charlotte cap having a ruffled border of lace with blue silk trimmed lace froth at front. 3" shoulder width. 10" length. Circa 1895.

367. White Cotton Pinafore Dress
Of fine white cotton muslin, the frock has open back that buttons to waist, fitted bodice with vertical tucks and scalloped-edge Bertha collar with embroidered detail, fitted waist, full gathered skirt with three rows of tucks, scalloped edge hem with overcast stitching, matching pockets, long sleeves with set-in cuffs trimmed to match the hem. 2 1/2" shoulder width. 6 1/2" waist. 7" length. Circa 1900.

368. Petite Pale Rose Cotton Frock
Rose cotton muslin frock with dropped waist that blousons in front, and fits snugly in the back, wide-pleated skirt with cotton lace trim, wide Bertha collar with lace edging, lace yoke and fitted collar, 3/4 length sleeves, ivory silk bow. 2" shoulder width. 7" hips. 5" length. Circa 1900.

369. Tiny White Pique Frock
Of vertically-ribbed white pique with fitted bodice trimmed with cutwork bretelles and cutwork band at yoke, wide sleeves with cutwork and scalloped edging, flared skirt with Swiss embroidery scalloped hemline, button and loop closure. 1 1/2" shoulder width. 3 1/2" waist. 2 1/2" length. Circa 1890.

370. Two, Petite Cotton Frocks
Of pale blue or rose muslin cotton, each with fitted collar trimmed with lace, lace or ribbon banding, wide bretelles trimmed with ribbon and lace, short puffed sleeves with lace trim, lace skirt borders, button backs. 3 1/2" shoulder width. 8" waist. 6" length. Circa 1910.

371. White Dotted Swiss Frock
Of white dotted Swiss with dropped waist the frock has full-gathered bodice, fitted yoke with cutwork banding and ruffled cutwork Bertha collar, gathered hip band, cutwork ruffled trim at hemline, puffed sleeves with lace edging, ivory silk ribbons, buttons and button holes.
6" shoulder width. 17" hips. 15" length. Circa 1900.

372. Sheer Cotton Voile Frock
Of white cotton voile with shadow-stripes and shaded mauve leafs and dots, dropped waist with blouson top, gathered skirt, 3/4 length very full sleeves with deep ruffles and lace edging, wide ruffled self collar with cording, muslin-lined bodice, button closure. 5" shoulder width. 15" drop waist. 15" length. Circa 1910.

373. Sheer Voile Frock with Detached Collar and Bonnet
Delicately-woven voile with interwoven dots comprises a high-waisted frock with woven design, full gathered skirt, full gathered sleeves with wide cutwork ruffle, insertion borders of cutwork, matching sash ties. With detachable wide Bertha collar, and double-ruffled wide brim, long ties. 6" shoulder width. 13" length. Circa 1900.

374. Aqua Silk Dropped Waist Frock
Sheer aqua/cream window pane silk frock over blue cotton underdress has dropped waist, diagonally-shaped bodice with silk covered buttons, lace-covered yoke with band collar, wide collar draping onto sleeves with silk passementerie trim, puffed sleeves with matching trim, silk sash, hook and eye closure. 6" shoulder width. 20" hips. 14" length. Circa 1915.

375. Ensemble of White Batiste in Original Box
Includes delicate white frock with narrow tucks and cutwork center-panel bodice, capelet sleeves with scalloped edges and embroidered flowers, set-in tatted waistband, lightly-gathered skirt with narrow horizontal tucks and scalloped embroidered hem, rose bows at shoulders, button back. With two matching slips, knit stockings, Charlotte bonnet with soft crown, pleated wide-brim, rose silk bow. In original box with rose paper edging, tulle-edged box interior, early engraving on lid with child holding doll. 4" shoulder width. 8" length. Circa 1885.

376. Two Silk Bonnets
Each designed to fit the back of head, with ruffles extending around the face; one of aqua silk satin with pleated back and brim, muslin lining; other of rose twill silk with feather-stitching at back of head, gathered brim at top of head, striped silk ribbon, muslin lining. To fit about 5" head width. Circa 1890.

377. Cream Patterned Cotton Frock with Undergarments
Of sheer cream cotton with interwoven stripes printed with delicately-shaded rosebuds, the frock has fitted yoke above a gathered bodice, set-in waistband, gathered skirt with gathered and lace-trimmed ruffle, 3/4 length full sleeves with ruffled lace trim, lined yoke, hook and eye closure. Included with undergarments comprising muslin chemise, pantalets with draw-string waist, petticoat and coutil cotton stays. 5" shoulder width. 13" waist. 12" length. Circa 1900.

377A. White Batiste Cutwork Frock with Bonnet
Finely-woven white frock with re-embroidered cutwork designs has V-shaped neckline, wide sleeves, set-in waist and simple gathered skirt, rose muslin underliner. With rose batiste wire-framed bonnet having pleats, lace trim, floral monture. And matching underslip. 7" shoulder width. 14" waist. 14" length. Circa 1920.

377B. Cream Cotton Frock with Interwoven Rose Bands
Of fine cream loosely-woven cotton with interwoven bands of rose suggesting ribbon-inserted-lace and overall printed design of tiny rosebuds, the dress has fitted yoke, box-pleated blouson-style bodice that covers the set-in waistband with tiny pleats and cording, gathered skirt, very full sleeves with dart-shaping at interior elbows, lace ruffled cuffs, lace at neckline and yoke, muslin-lined bodice, hook and eye closure. 5" shoulder width. 15" dropped waist. 11" length. Circa 1900.

378. White Cotton Twill Frock with Blue Dots
Of sturdily-woven white twill with tiny blue dots, the shift-style frock has set-in yoke of cotton cutwork with scalloped edging, full bishop sleeves with wide ruffled cutwork borders and feather-stitch trim, narrow sewn-down pleats to waist, pressed-down pleats below the detached matching hip belt, belt loops, button closure. 5" shoulder width. 13" length.

378A. Three-Piece Black Woolen Spanish Costume
Of thickly-woven rich black wool the ensemble comprises matador-style jacket with rounded collar, slit pockets, double-seamed long sleeves, black cotton lining, cord loop closures; matching sleeveless vest with cotton lining and backing, loop closures, slip pockets; and matching slim pants with button-fly front, two front pockets. Each piece elaborately trimmed with narrow white soutache braid. 9" shoulder width. 17" waist. 19" pants length. Circa 1895.

378B. Blue and White Gingham Romper Suit
Of tiny blue and white checkered gingham, the suit comprises long tunic top with flared sides, two sewn-down tucks on either side, short form-fitting sleeves, button back, and matching knickers with chemise top and elastic leg bands. With matching muslin collar, tie, cuffs, and sash with decorative bands. 6" shoulder width. 14" tunic length. 10" waist. Circa 1920.

378C. Blue Cotton Chambray Romper Suit and Bonnet
Of pale blue cotton chambray the one-piece suit has square-cut neckline, short sleeves with banded cuffs, sewn-down bodice tucks for shaping, bloomer-style legs with elastic at leg bottoms, trimmed with banding and cord in manner to suggest bib. With matching sunbonnet having wide brim with turned-back flaps, twill brim liner, muslin ties, button closure. 6" shoulder width. Circa 1920.

379. Cotton Shift with Contrasting Trim
Of white cotton with printed blue pattern, the simple shift frock has rounded neckline with detached collar and tie of blue twill, sleeveless with blue twill banding at armholes, blue twill sash, belt loops. 6" shoulder width. 11" length. Circa 1920.

380. White Cotton Twill Sailor Dress and Pants
Of white twill, the A-line frock has button front with faux-box-pleat placket, double-breasted buttons, rounded collar with blue cord edging, short puffed sleeves with turn-up cuffs and blue banding, embroidered blue anchor, attached waist ties. With matching pants. 5" shoulders. 9" length. Circa 1930.

381. Brown Print Linen Frock
Of light-brown linen printed with contrasting stripes in darker brows and narrow patterned stripes, the frock has inverted V-shaped yoke with built-in sleeves, roll-up cuffs, dress front and back with sewn-down narrow pleats on either side of centered box pleat, detachable small collar, hip belt and belt loops. The collar, tie, cuffs and belt with applied red woven braid, snap closure. 5" shoulders. 12" length. 14" hips. Circa 1925.

382. Doll Socks and Mittens
In various colors and styles, each commercially woven, comprising three pairs of "B" woven socks, one pair of "B" woven mittens, and four additional pairs of socks with black detailed borders. Circa 1900.

383. Four Pairs of Doll Shoes
In various styles, colors and sizes, suitable for German dolls. Including red leather with scalloped edges (2 1/2" L.), brown leather with ankle straps and black heels (3"), brown leather saddle shoes signed "Made in Germany" (2 1/4"), and metallic-brown leather shoes with leather and silver bows, ankle straps with bronzed button, size 4, (3"). Circa 1900.

Chapter VIII

Chemises and Undergarments
1870 - 1915

384. Rose Cotton Muslin Chemise Frock
Of highly-sized rose cotton muslin with muslin-lined snugly-fitted bodice overlaid with wide matching bretelles trimmed with lace and ribbons, taupe lace on yoke, fitted neckline, 3/4 gathered sleeves with fitted cuffs, full skirt with tucks and ruffled border. 3 1/2" shoulder width. 8" waist. 10" overall. Circa 1900.

385. Red Sateen Chemise Frock
Of rose cotton sateen with full muslin-lining, the frock has snugly-fitted bodice with overlaid same-fabric bretelles trimmed with lace and braid, and centering the cream sateen vest front, gathered yoke, sateen fitted neckline, 3/4 sleeves, slightly-gathered skirt, leather belt. 4" shoulder width. 8 1/2" waist. 10" overall. Circa 1900.

386. Red Cotton Twill Chemise Frock
High-waist cotton twill frock with cream pleated bodice, red pleated skirt and 1/2 length sleeves, very wide detached Bertha collar trimmed with braid and very wide border of pleated Alencon lace with insertion edging, matching lace at skirt. 4" shoulder width. 8 1/2" waist. 10" overall. Circa 1900.

387. Blue Cotton Sateen Store-Frock
Of pale blue cotton sateen with full muslin lining, the frock has box-pleated bodice front, 1/2 length full sleeves with sateen brocade cuffs, matching sateen brocade collar and sash, passementerie trim on collar and bodice, attached sateen tie, gathered skirt. 4" shoulder width. 8" waist. 9" overall length. Circa 1900.

388. White Muslin Chemise Frock
Loosely-fitted with box-pleats at center front, set-in narrow-pleated yoke edged by cotton-lace trimmed narrow bretelles, matching lace at neckline, 3/4 length full sleeves. 4" shoulder width. 11" overall. Circa 1900.

389. Blue Patterned Sateen Store Frock
High-waisted, with snugly-fitted fully-lined bodice overlaid by Bertha collar trimmed with double row of braid, cotton lace collar, short full sleeves, gathered skirt, silk ribbons. 2 1/2" shoulder width. 5" waist. 6" overall length. Circa 1900.

390. White Muslin Nightgown
Of thickly-woven muslin, the nightgown has set-in yoke, rounded neckline with wide ruffled collar having cutwork and scalloped-edge trim, long full sleeves with set-in cuffs trimmed with feather-stitch and ruffled cutwork, long full gown with cartridge pleating at the yoke. 8" shoulder width. 23" length. Circa 1885.

391. White Muslin Nightgown with Red Trim
Of thickly-woven muslin, the princess-styled nightgown has rounded neckline with stand-up collar, inverted box pleats to hips, 3/4 length sleeves with wide loose set-in cuffs, set-in yoke at back with gathers below, red cord edges the collar, front placket opening and cuffs. 8" shoulder width. 24" length. Circa 1885.

392. Blue Chambray Petticoat
Of blue chambray, the petticoat has set-in waistband with button, handmade button-holes, thick red cotton lace at hem, leaf and geometric red embroidery trim on the gathered skirt. 11" waist. Circa 1890.

393. White Pique Baby Jacket and Bib
Of white vertically-banded pique, the snugly-fitted jacket has 3/4 sleeves, scalloped-edge rounded collar and turn-up cuffs with embroidered detail, button back. With elongated bib of rich cutwork and embroidery, button-back-neck. 4" shoulder width. Circa 1885.

394. White Cotton Marseilles Baby Jacket and Bib
Of heavy white ribbed cotton with inside layer of flannel fleece, the fitted jacket has set-in sleeves with gathered cuffs, front band with cotton lace and button trim, hidden button and loop closure, cording and cotton lace collar trim. With elongated bib of flannel-back Marseille cotton and Swiss embroidery. 4 1/2" shoulder width. Circa 1885.

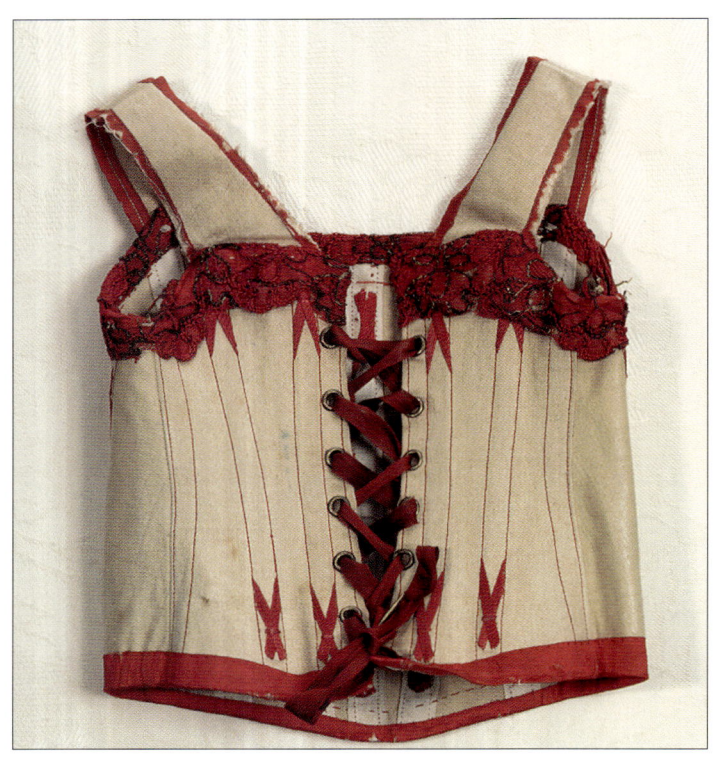

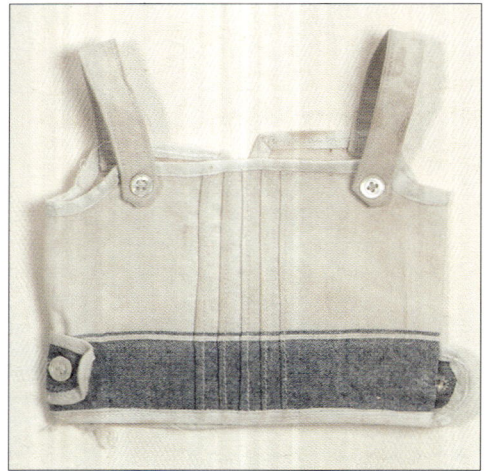

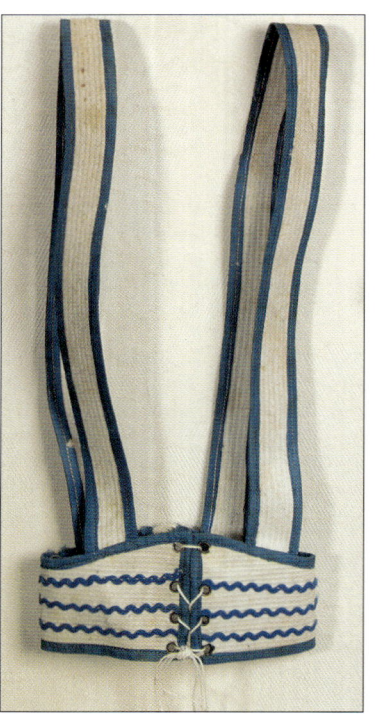

395. Cotton Coutil Boned Bebe Stays with Red Silk Embroidery
Of light-brown cotton coutil, the corset has six built-in bone supports, further set-in ribbed panels, graduated-width shoulder straps, brass grommets for lacing, pearl buttons at straps and for attachment to petticoat, and is decorated with red silk embroidery, red cotton lace and banding, stamped "Orleans (and other illegible word)" on interior. 13" waist. French, circa 1890.

396. Blue Cotton Sateen Bebe Stays
Of powder-blue cotton sateen with full muslin lining, V-shaped stitching at front bodice, shoulder straps, brass grommet lacing holes, lace trim, buttons for attachment to petticoat. 9" waist. Circa 1890.

397. White Cotton Leading Strings
Of ribbed white cotton, the wide waist-band has two elongated shoulder straps, brass grommet lacing holes at back, blue cotton banding, and blue rick-rack trim hand-basted to waist-band. Ink-inscribed reference on interior. 9" waist. Circa 1875.

398. Cream/Indigo Muslin Bebe Stays
Wide woven muslin panels of cream and blue indigo are constructed in wrap-around bebe stays fashion, with button back, shoulder straps, vertical front tucks, cotton banding at all edges and a decorative very narrow band at the junction of blue and cream. 12" waist. Circa 1880.

399. Peach Cotton Twill Bebe Stays
Peach cotton twill with contrasting cream cotton twill lining has vertically-ribbed stitching supports, narrow shoulder straps, cotton banding, lace trim, four pairs of lacing grommets, buttons for attachment to petticoats. 8" waist. Circa 1885.

400. Ivory Sateen Corset for Lady Doll
Of fine lustrous sateen with dull reverse, the corset has elongated torso, waist definition, bone-insertions, straps, hook and eye closure, wide band of lace trimmed with blue silk ribbons. 8" waist. Circa 1890.

401. White Cambric Chemisette and Corset
Of sturdy tightly-woven cambric cotton, the chemisette has square-cut low neckline, short slightly-puffed sleeves, fullness at bodice, set-in waistband, trimming of broderie anglaise and bands of insertion embroidery, back buttons/buttons holes; with boned corset having lacing bands at front and back, lace borders, unusual blue and white woven pattern. 6 1/2" shoulder width. Circa 1900.

402. Twill "Corsetine" for Lady Doll, with Patent Date
Of very sturdy twill, the lady's corset has strapless top with scalloped cotton lace edging, elongated length to fit over hips with built-in elastic gussets at waist and hips, lacing closure at front, metal hooks at back, stamped label "Corsetine/Gown Attachment/Pat. Dec. 19, 1899". 8 1/2" waist. Circa 1900.

403. Embroidered Sateen Bebe Stays with Maker's Label
Of cream cotton sateen with woven-embroidered floral pattern in orange and green, orange silk banding and shoulder straps, four brass grommet lacing holes, muslin lining, stamped "Corsets Felix Pere 12 rue Saint-Rome, Toulouse, Reclame Deposee". 8" waist. Circa 1890.

404. Sand-Sateen Boned Corset
Of sand-colored cotton sateen, the strapless corset has eleven set-in bone supports, six pairs of brass lacing grommets, blue silk ribbon and insertion lace at bodice and waist. 8" waist. Circa 1885.

405. Five White Cotton Blouses
Of various styles, each with button back, set-in sleeves, rounded necklines. With various trims including tucks, lace, embroidery. 5" - 9" shoulder width. Circa 1865-1890.

406. Three-Piece White Cotton Undergarments
Of fine white muslin cotton, comprising full slip with lace-trimmed neckline and sleeves, drawstring waist; petticoat with set-in waistband and double-tiered gathered skirt; and pantalets with set-in waistband. Each trimmed with multiple rows of tucks and lace borders. 6 1/2" shoulder width. 9" waist. 9" petticoat length. Circa 1910.

407. Four-Piece Crisp Muslin Ensemble
Of sheer highly-starched muslin, comprising chemise with draw-string neckline having high lace collar, long full sleeves with drawstring lace-trimmed cuffs; petticoat with set-in waistband, flat front, gathered back, rows of tucks, featherstitching and ribbon-drawn lace at hemline; pantalets with set-in waistband, lace trimmed cuffs with drawn ribbons; apron constructed of bands of lace with drawn ribbon. 6" waist. 6" petticoat length. Circa 1890.

137

408. Set, Lace Collar and Cuffs on Original Paper
Of finely-woven openwork lace, the rounded collar and cuffs have scalloped picot edging, are still stitched onto their original blue paper. 4" width cuffs. Circa 1885.

409. Undergarments and Shoes for S.F.B.J. Size 8
Comprising muslin one-piece undergarment with high-waisted chemise top and attached pants, with attached pleated slip front and back, the slip opens at the sides for free-movement. With matching nylon stockings with attached garters, and white leather shoes with white overcast edging, cut-hole decorative edging, silk ties, white leather soles signed "S.F.B.J. Paris 8". 8" shoulder width. Circa 1915.

409A. Pique Bebe Stays and Bloomers
The cotton-lined pique bebe stays with vertical ribbing have metal-grommet-lacing holes, cord ties, cotton straps, buttons to attach to cotton bloomers with cutwork scalloped embroidery. 6" shoulder width. 12" waist. Circa 1885.

Chapter IX

Mariner Costumes
1880 - 1915

410. Petite Red Wool Flannel Mariner Costume
Of sturdy red wool flannel, the dropped-waist jacket dress has faux-jacket bodice with centered sewn-down pleats below a red flannel yoke, sailor collar, sewn-in wide waistband, gathered skirt, long sleeves with fullness at shoulders and set-in cuffs. The costume is trimmed with double rows of wide and narrow ivory herringbone-woven trim on collar, bodice, waist, skirt and cuffs, little silver anchor pin. 2 1/2" shoulder width. 6" loose waist. 5" length. Circa 1885.

411. Petite Two-Piece Navy Jersey Mariner Costume
Of dark navy cotton jersey, the outfit comprises blouse with rounded neckline, sewn-down collar, long sleeves, button back with little brass buttons; and skirt with cotton muslin to hips, draw-string waist, pleated jersey below the hips. The blouse and skirt are trimmed with wide white braid at collar, cuffs, hips and hem. 3" shoulder width. 7" hips. 3 1/2" skirt length. Circa 1885.

412. Navy Blue Wool Three-Piece Mariner Ensemble
Of sturdy navy blue wool, the ensemble comprises jacket with front opening, wide sailor collar, breast pocket, silk tie, and long sleeves with unusual dart-shaping at wrists and hook and eye wrist closure; flared-shape pleated skirt with wide front box pleat, hook and eye closure; and matching beret cap. All pieces are trimmed with triple rows of narrow white piping. 5" shoulder width. 10" waist. 9" skirt length. Circa 1885.

413. Navy Blue Twill Mariner Dress and Jacket
Of sturdy navy blue twill, the ensemble comprising dropped-waist sleeveless dress with navy blue cotton

sateen bodice having stitched-down pale blue cotton center panel trimmed with double rows of narrow white piping, navy blue twill pleated skirt; and navy blue twill jacket with cotton sateen lining, double row of tiny brass decorative buttons, sleeves with dart-shaped cuffs, pale blue rounded collar trimmed with triple row of white piping and pleated white cotton edging. The ensemble presented in its original gift box with lithograph of girl at seashore on the lid. 5 1/2" shoulder width. 15" hips. 14" dress length. Circa 1895.

414. Three-Piece Mariner-Style Jacket Of navy blue wool flannel or serge, each with pale blue cotton middy collar trimmed with narrow bands of white piping; one with matching blue cuffs and drawstring waist; two others with cotton lining, sewn-down pleats at cuffs for snug fitting, and double row of tiny brass buttons. Each about 4" shoulder width. Circa 1885.

416. White Cotton Pique Boy's Sailor Costume
Of sturdy white cotton pique, the two-piece ensemble comprises pull-over sailor jacket with straight side, wide sailor collar with placket opening at front, sleeves to wrist, scalloped-edge embroidered cutwork cotton trim at collar and cuffs; with matching short pants having cartridge pleating at set-in waistband which is adjustable by drawstrings. 4 1/2" shoulder width. 8" adjustable waist. 5" L. of shorts. Circa 1885.

417. Black and Ivory Two-Piece Mariner Costume
Of an exceptional vertically-ribbed fabric with alternating ribs of narrowly-ribbed black velvet and cream silk, the ensemble comprises short fitted jacket with front opening, double row of brass buttons, wide sailor collar, full sleeves with fitted cuffs, the collar and cuffs trimmed with a double row of cutwork lace; and sleeveless dress with white cotton top trimmed with lace at neckline and shoulders, button back, pleated skirt to match jacket. 3 1/2" shoulder width. 9" hips. 9" overall length. Circa 1885.

418. White Cotton Pique Mariner Dress
Of thickly woven, vertically-ribbed white pique, the one-piece dress has dropped waist, blouson top, hidden front hook and eye closure, 3/4 sleeves with set-in cuffs, modified sailor collar with square-cut ends and inset cotton trim, pleated skirt below the hips, hip sash. 5 1/2" shoulder width. 14" hips. 11" length. Circa 1890.

419. White Cotton Pique Two-Piece Mariner Costume
Of narrow-horizontally-ribbed white cotton twill, the ensemble comprises sleeveless dress with white cotton bodice and hip belt, above pique pleated skirt with four bands of narrow braid and border of looped braid. With matching hip-length blouson jacket, button front, coat sleeves with double seams and turn-up decorative cuffs, sailor collar trimmed with border of broderie anglaise. 5 1/2" shoulder width. 14" hips. 12" dress length. Circa 1882.

415. White Cotton Pique Mariner Dress and Jacket
Of narrow-ribbed white pique, the ensemble comprises dress whose center bodice panel of pique is flanked by sides and back of lightweight cotton, rounded neckline, button back, fully box-pleated skirt; with matching sailor jacket cut with slightly-flared sides, front opening with single hidden button and double row of decorative buttons, wide sailor collar with 1" border of scalloped cutwork cotton trim, coat-style sleeves cut very full at shoulders and clasped at the wrist by sewn-down pleats, two rows of thick braid down each front jacket panel. 7" shoulder width. 16" hips. 16" dress length. Circa 1885.

420. Red Wool Mariner Costume with Matching Cap
The ensemble comprises red wool pullover middy blouse with detachable matching yoke, sailor collar trimmed with black silk piping, breast pocket with slit opening, long sleeves with fitted cuffs trimmed with black piping, unusual fold-over at jacket bottom with decorative buttons. With matching black wool knickers constructed with pressed-down pleats from set-in waistband to set-in knee cuffs, constructed crotch gusset, snap closure at both sides of waist. With matching black linen sailor cap having flat top, black grosgrain band, silk lining. 6 1/2" shoulder width. 9" middy length. 12" waist. Circa 1900.

421. Two-Piece Navy Blue Wool Boy's Sailor Suit
Of very lightweight navy blue wool, the ensemble comprises hip-length jacket with button front, rounded sailor collar with white cording, detachable yoke with white

stitching, embroidered white anchor, double-seamed short sleeves with white cording, silver buttons, detachable matching belt. And matching knickers with gathering below the knees, drawstring waist. 8" shoulder width. 13" jacket length. 16" adjustable waist. Circa 1910.

422. Two Woolen Sailor Caps
Each in classic sailor style with soft flat tops, shaped banding designed to sit just at crown of head; comprising red wool cap with red grosgrain ribbon gold stencilled "Marceau", and red pompoms, 3" inside brim width. And navy blue cap embroidered with white anchor, blue silk band with gold stenciling "Mignon" and white muslin lining, 2" inside brim width. Circa 1900.

423. Two Leather Sailor Caps
Each in soft kid leather in classic sailor style with flat tops, shaped banding, comprising light-tan cap with brown grosgrain ribbon band having gold stenciling "Mignon", green silk twill lining, 5" inside brim width. And dark brown leather with brown silk ribbon stencilled "Celine", green silk lining, 3" inside brim. Circa 1900.

424. White Wool Boy's Sailor Suit with Cap
Of lightweight white wool, the three-piece ensemble comprises short-sleeved middy top with button front, wide sailor collar, detachable yoke with embroidered navy blue anchor, short sleeves, detachable belt, blue braid trim at collar, belt and sleeves; with matching white wool knickers, and matching blue wool sailor cap with flat-top, white grosgrain ribbon band labelled in gold "Lutin", and white decorative ribbon and pompom, black silk lining. 7" shoulder width. 4 1/2" inside brim. Circa 1915.

425. White Wool and Navy Boy's Sailor Suit for Bebe Jumeau
The two-piece ensemble comprises lightweight white wool middy blouse with short sleeves having turn-up navy blue cuffs, sailor collar with V-shaped navy blue wool applique, faux-double breasted with decorative pearl buttons, hook and eye closure; button attachment to muslin-lined navy blue wool shorts. The blouse is trimmed with narrow bands of grosgrain white or blue ribbon, blue silk tie. "11" tag inside collar designates sizing for Bebe Jumeau 11. Circa 1915.

426. Two-Piece Navy Wool Sailor Dress and Coat
Of tightly-woven navy wool, the one-piece sailor dress has shaped fitted yoke with detachable center panel, slit breast pocket, loosely-falling pleats from the yoke with wide center box pleats, matching hip belt, long sleeves with gathered fitted cuffs and fitting dart at elbows, black silk tie, triple bands of narrow white piping on collar and cuffs. And matching double-breasted coat with cream silk lining, brass buttons at front and cuffs, pockets with front flaps, red embroidered beaver symbol of Canada on coat sleeve. With original boutique label "Fashionable Store, T.D. Dubuc, 188 to 198 St. John St. Quebec". 7" shoulders. 15" overall length. Circa 1920.

427. Navy Twill Three-Piece Mariner-Style Costume
Of navy cotton twill, the ensemble comprises hip-length flared jacket with coat collar, notched lapels, faux double-breasted front with double row of brass buttons, faux pockets with tiny flaps, double-seamed coat sleeves with sewn-down fitting darts at cuffs, full silk lining. With matching flared skirt having inverted box pleat at center back, suspender straps, set-in waist, hook and eye closure. And matching beret with black silk lining and band having gold stencilled "U.S.S. Olympic". 7" shoulder width. 15" waist. 17" coat length. Circa 1915.

428. Navy Blue Wool Hooded Coat, with Matching Red Knit Accessories
Of navy blue wool, the double-breasted coat has long double-seamed sleeves with black and red flannel epaulets, red piping trim, rounded collar with red lining and piping, matching gathered-edge hood hidden under the collar, red flannel lining, two pockets with red piping, double row of brass buttons with embossed anchor. With red knit cap, mittens, short leggings, and neck scarf. 7" shoulder width. 10" leggings waist. 15" length.

429. Mariner Cap "Normandie" in Original Store Box
Of dark navy blue wool, the flat-topped sailor cap has hidden wire frame at outer edge, firmly-shaped band decorated with navy blue grosgrain ribbon having gold-lettering "Normandie", pale blue cotton sateen lining. Presented in original navy blue box with lithograph of young boy in sailor suit on the lid. 5" inside head width. Circa 1890.

Chapter X

Miscellaneous Costumes Including Gentlemens, Occupational and Folklore
1875 - 1925

**431. Emerald Green
Top Hat with French Label**
Of brushed rich green plush, with firm top and brim, green silk grosgrain band, green silk lining, original gilt stencilled lettering and symbol of angel head, "Alphonsine, 15 rue de la Paix, Paris". 2" head width. Circa 1890.

432. Gentleman's Formalwear Suit
Of black serge, the ensemble comprises trousers with fly-front, long-sleeved jacket with rolled collar, satin lapels, silk lining; three-button vest with rolled collar, silk backing, and brown muslin lining; and highly-starched shirt front with narrow tucks, stand-up collar and bow tie, pearl buttons; separate cuffs with gold-plated cuff pins, and faux pocket watch with fob. 6" shoulder width. Circa 1900.

437. Cotton Khaki Military Uniform
Of dark cotton khaki, the uniform comprises simple collarless jacket with four faux pocket flaps, long sleeves, brass buttons; with short pants having hemmed legs, drawstring waist; white muslin shirt with button front and collar, khaki cap, leather leggings and shoes. (Also long cape and larger cap of identical material included). 4 1/2 shoulder width of jacket. Circa 1915.

433. Gentleman's Top Coat, Trousers, Shirt
The topcoat of grey flannel wool with double-breasted front, lapels, black velvet collar, black velvet buttons and cuffs, long double-seamed coat sleeves, breast pocket, back vent, top-stitching. With white long-sleeved shirt having button holes in front for "diamond" studs, and long black wool trousers. 4" shoulder width. 8" waist. 13" coat length. Circa 1890.

434. Man's Black Wool Jacket and Vest
Of soft black woolen fabric, the set comprises open-front jacket with unusual double-tiered lappets extending below the waist and trimmed with brass buttons, black silk banding around all outside edges, silk lining, long sleeves with turn-up cuffs; and matching vest with V-shape waist, black silk banding, brass buttons, muslin lining and back. 4 1/2" shoulders. 9" waist. Circa 1900.

435. Boy's Woolen Sport Cap with Original Label
Of thick wool tweed, the soft-crowned cap has fir-fronted brim which snap-attaches to cap, brown muslin lining with original label, comprising illustration of tennis player and "Le Reve du Sportman, Cap's Tennis, Grand Luxe". 3" head width. Circa 1910.

436. Priest Costume
Of ivory brocade silk and yellow silk, muslin and black cotton, comprising the following elements: manipole, stole, amice, chasuble, cincture, alb, and three-piece cassock worn under silk robes or when not in mass. Each piece constructed in authentic detail including hand-screened symbols, tassels, fringe, lace. About 3 1/2" shoulder width. Circa 1885.

438. Traditional Bridal Costume of Northern Europe
Comprising long-sleeved white cotton blouse with stand-up collar, placket and cuffs of cutwork linen with picot edging, black challis skirt with orange trim at hemline, red wool vest with gold thread and black cording edging, richly-embroidered bodice front, white apron with red wool sash having glass bead trim, red wool cap with glass bead trim, petticoat, pantalets, orange stockings (sewn onto original body in original manner). 3 1/2" shoulder width. 9" waist. 12" body length. Circa 1900.

439. Traditional Costume of Eastern Europe
Comprising black woolen jumper with V-shaped high yoke having red piping and multi-colored embroidered flowers, gathered skirt; matching black cotton apron with black wool embroidered sash; black wool embroidered matching cap; one-piece muslin undergarments; white cotton shirt with lace trimmed collar and cuffs; one-piece undergarment; orange cotton stockings, black leather shoes. 4" shoulder width. 8" yoke circumference. 8" overall length. 1 3/4" L. shoes. Circa 1915.

440. Traditional Exotic Costume of Silk Brocade
Comprising sheer silk tunic with interwoven silk shadow stripe and blue silk bands, edging of hand-made blue silk rick-rack, long pagoda-shaped lace and metallic sleeves; blue and gold brocade silk tunic with very short sleeves, rounded neckline with gold cord and gold decorative buttons, patterned silk linings; crimson silk brocade harem-style pants with tiny leg openings and bloomer legs, drawstring waist; and cream silk hooded cape with fringe trim. 4 1/2" shoulder width. 8" adjustable waist. 9" tunic length. Circa 1885.